The Palace and Gardens of Fronteira

JOSÉ CASSIANO NEVES

The Palace and Gardens of Fronteira

SEVENTEENTH & EIGHTEENTH CENTURY PORTUGUESE STYLE

Third revised edition by

Vera Mendes and Fernando Mascarenhas

Photography by Nicolas Sapieha

DISTRIBUTED BY
ANTIQUE COLLECTOR'S CLUB

WAPPINGER'S FALLS, NEW YORK   WOODBRIDGE, ENGLAND

The publishers wish to thank the Fundação das Casas
de Fronteira e Alorna for their help in making this book possible.

First published in the United States of America
in 1995 by Quetzal Editores,
Fernando Mascarenhas, M.T. Train/Scala Books

Design by Rogério Petinga
Color separations by Multitipo (Queluz)
Printed and bound by
Sfera International, Milano

ISBN: 0-9357-48-98-90

Index

A Note from the Editors   7

A brief history   9

The Palace   28

    Sala das Batalhas   35

    Library   47

    Torrinha Sul   51

    Gallery   54

    Sala dos Painéis   58

    Sala de Juno or Sala Império   66

    Sala dos Quatro Elementos   70

    Sala de Eros   71

    Sala das Quatro Estações or Sala de Fumo   71

    The Bedroom   71

    The Terrace outside the Chapel   74

    Chapel   81

The Gardens   83

The Mascarenhas Lords and Founders of this Palace   104

Rococo Stuccoes and Tiles in the Palace of Fronteira   127

by José Meco

Mural paintings at the Palace of Fronteira   133

by Mafalda Osório

Notes   139

Detail of a griffon in a wall painting in the Sala Imperio. Below: detail of stucco work in the Sala das Batalhas.

A Note from the Editors

The editors thought it would be useful to the reader to present some corrections and addenda to this work by Professor Neves.

These corrections and addenda are of several kinds. To begin with, Professor Neves's work on the subject of this book continued over the years, during which time he accumulated a number of important annotations to his original text. These seemed indispensible to this third edition, as did the corrections, made possible by recent historical investigation, of several inaccuracies in the text: inaccuracies that Professor Neves himself would most certainly have wanted cleared up. It also seemed appropriate, given the author's preference for clarity, to enrich the work's accuracy inasmuch as this was possible without affecting its coherence as a whole.

Finally, it seemed to the editors that the work would be enriched by the inclusion of a number of texts by José Meco and Mafalda Osório covering different aspects of the same subject matter.

A brief history

I

Façade of the Palace, viewed from the tank of the Galeria dos Reis. Once an open loggia, today it is closed and its windows belong to the library of the Palace flanked by the north and south towers.

In São Domingos de Benfica Square, at the foot of the Monsanto hills, lies the former Convent of São Domingos, of the Order of Pregadores (preachers). The quinta had belonged to the Marquises of Abrantes and later to Regent Infanta Isabel Maria, who «at one time established a small court there»[1]. The property then passed to the Marquises of Fronteira. Having been so well preserved, it is today considered one of Portugal's most unique monuments.

In spite of being such a small place, it has many memories and tells much of our past through the people who lived and died there and the historical events which took place there.

In 1399 Dom João I donated an old quinta and small houses which he owned in Benfica to the Order of Pregadores at the request of the jurist, João das Regras, and of Frei Vicente, the King's confessor. The convent was «totally rebuilt early in the seventeenth century»[2]. The church, remarkable for its beautiful seventeenth-century tiling [by António de Oliveira Bernardes], and for its magnificent woodcarvings and holy images, was the Fronteira's pantheon. This also included sepulchral inscriptions of some of the more distinguished members of this family, as well as those of many other important Portuguese.

There we can find, amongst others, the tombs of Frei Luís de Sousa, who took his religious vows there and died in 1632; Frei Vicente, preacher to Dom João I, Sergeant-Major Manuel Carrião de Castanheda, and Vasco Martins de Albergaria, chamberlain to Prince Henry the Navigator. Mid-choir, one also finds «the tomb (national monument) of Dom João das Regras (d.1404). The statue shows the famous jurist lying down, wearing a robe, cap, and wide buttoned collar, holding a book over his chest, and with his wavy hair falling over his forehead»[3].

Also noteworthy is the Castros Chapel (national monument) situated in the convent's cloister, «dating from the first half of the seventeenth century»[4]. Viceroy Dom João de Castro, his wife, and many other members of this family's tombs can be seen here — hence its name.

Built in the mid-eighteenth century in the Marquis of Pombal's time «by Stephane Devisme, businessman and capitalist»[5] the quinta of the Marquises of Abrantes is interesting for its «gardens with boxwood benches, trees clipped into the shapes of vases, sunshades, and banisters. Also present are ponds, waterfalls, busts and several statues (featuring Flora, Ceres, Mercury, Venus, Pomona, and others) some of them signed (by artists such as Pandetti, Danieletti, and Gabbani)»[6].

In the Palace with its interesting stucco work and ceilings thought to be painted by Pillement and Cirilo Wolkmar Machado, lived the Infanta Isabel Maria. She became Regent upon the death of Dom João VI, from 6th March 1826 until 22nd February 1828, when she handed the powers over to Dom Miguel.

Frei Luís de Sousa,[7] in S. Domingo's chronicle referring to this place, said «a mere league from the city on the road to Sintra and a little to the west from it, lies, hidden away from human communication, a small valley which has a natural pleasantness because of its fresh springs and trees, with the name of Benfica... From all sides run quintas which surround the hills and valleys, some of good construction, others less: all rich in woods and orchards and surrounded by their vineyards, with which the valley keeps its fresh and eternal greenness throughout the year». De Sousa did not refer to any particular quinta and obviously not to the quinta of the Marquises of Fronteira, which at that time did not exist — at least not in this splendor. However it was already worthy of notice in the early eighteenth century, as Father Carvalho da Costa[8]

A sepia photograph made at the end of the nineteenth-century, showing the north façade of the Palace.

An engraving from the nineteenth -century representing the fenced enclosure with sculpture of Mars and Venus on either side of the gate.
Opposite page, the garden and east façade appear lozenge-shaped in a late nineteenth century engraving.

talking of the parish of Benfica, mentions that «The renowned quinta of the Marquises of Fronteira is in this parish...»

[In the late eighteen hundreds, Ramalho Ortigão[9] wrote the following: «Although so fallen from its former importance in the fickle and capricious opinions of the capital's high society, the old and friendly town of Benfica is still a little suburban retreat from Lisbon. It carries the same prestige that Tivoli and Frascati must hold for Rome. In no other place in Portugal, with the exception of Sintra, can there be found in so small an area such beautiful, historical, anecdotal and nostalgic quintas as in Benfica... They approach, nearly joining in a sweet murmur of water, splashing in the springs or running and bubbling into the dripping garden earth. Orchards and vegetable gardens, in a perennial greenness of rural and luxurious vegetation, give forth a bucolic perfume, as do the flowers and fruits. The quintas belonged to the Marquis of Fronteira, the Count of Farrobo, and the Marquises of Abrantes, and later to the Infanta Isabel Maria, previously of Lodi, to Beau Séjour, to the dead Baron de Glória, and many others».

The suburban 'villa' of ancient Rome began to spread from the Renaissance onwards. New social, economical and security conditions permitted the realization of the humanist ideal of the country house in which to rest the spirit. One of the most perfect architectural examples of this is that of the Villa Medici in Careggi, Florence.]

Thus «kings, monks, nobles and enriched bourgeois paraded their magnificence and hierarchical pomp» (Ramalho Ortigão), building majestic palaces for which the most important artists were summoned. [Or, as Santos Simões, Portugal's expert on tiles, tells us, «it is the new military and political aristocracy, with no professional worries, which leaps into construction or enlargement of palaces and which searches for 'modern' ornaments, giving parties where a new *joi de vivre* is apparent. The examples come from above, from important politicians and military men — the Saldanhas, the Albuquerques, the Mascarenhas...»[10].]

All that has been written about the Palace of the Marquises of Fronteira, shows that it is unsurpassed in value in the history of Portuguese architecture. We can confirm that in our country, so poor in monuments of this kind, there are few houses that can be compared to it, and even abroad it would always be worthy of notice.

To the beauty of its gardens, in Italian style, the magnificence of its Palace must be added. The latter is all the more admirable for having been built in an age when the great lords were more dedicated to warfare than to works of art.

In Portugal, luxury and richness were more associated with the religious orders upon which our kings' attentions were focused, than with the noble houses. As evidence of this, following the wars of Restoration there were «139 Holy Days in the Portuguese calendar, not counting those for processions and pilgrimages»[11].

Júlio de Castilho, in his beautiful work *Lisboa Antiga* [12], quoting a book by an anonymous author entitled *Voyage en Portugal en 1796*, referring to the nobles, remarks that «they are not great for their wealth, not for their luxury and magnificence, not even for their representation... Their palaces are only noteworthy for their size, architecture, ornamentation, and furniture. Everything is below what is used by people of medium richness... Their carriages are common, no better than two wheeled chaises; a few possess coaches, but they are ordinary and outmoded. The luxury of these gentlemen is to harness four mules, to be accompanied by a servant on horseback bearing a sword, whom they call valet, and to have a great number of servants...»

Clenardo [13], referring to these gentlemen riding out with a retinue of servants, wrote: «None lacks for work, although they lead a pampered life: two lead the group; the third carries the hat; the fourth the cape, in case it should rain; the fifth holds the beasts' reins; the sixth stays near the stirrups to hold the silk shoes; the seventh brings the brush to dust the clothes; the eighth has a cloth to clean the sweat off

The fifth Marquis de Fronteira, Dom José Luís de Mascarenhas, a detail from the stucco work in the Sala das Batalhas:

the animal, whilst their master hears mass or converses with a friend; the ninth gives him a comb if he has to greet somebody of importance, that he not appear with his wig disheveled».

This testimony by Count Raczynski[14] in *Les Arts au Portugal* is also interesting: «Les voyageurs du XVIe siècle, entre autres le cardinal Alexandrino, nonce du pape, ainsi que les ambassadeurs vénitiens, les chevaliers Tron et Lippomani, envoyés auprés de Philippe II d'Espagne pour le complimenter au sujet de la conquête du Portugal, expriment leur étonnement à cet égard dans le manuscrit intitulé: *Comentario per Italia, Francia, Spania e Portogallo, overo relazione del viaggio*. Ano 1581: copies faites d'aprés l'original de la bibliothèque du Vatican... Ces voyageurs disent qu'ils n'on pas rencontré en Portugal un seul Palais de grand seigneur, ayant un caractère architectonique determiné et régulier».

These are interesting impressions which add to the importance of this Palace, its founder and descendants who have enlarged and bettered it so much.

Shell work, stucco and tiling are three important decorative elements of this Palace. If it had nothing else, these would make a visit worthwhile, particularly the latter which «constituent en partie la physionomie de Portugal»[15].

Detail of the stucco work in the Sala das Batalhas.
At right, the entrance to the chapel has columns faced with tile, displaying grotesque, anthropomorphic images.

José Queirós's phrase referring to the Royal Palace in Sintra[16] can, without exaggeration, be applied to this house: «It is an authentic museum of tile work». Likewise the statement of Joaquim Rasteiro when he refers to the Palace of Bacalhoa[17]: «It is...a ceramics museum». A little further on, still on the same subject, José Queirós remarks on «the tile work of the Palace and gardens of the Marquises of Fronteira in São Domingos of Benfica, so interesting in ceramics and in history»[18].

[According to Santos Simões, «This house of the Mascarenhas offers a selection of tile work of the greatest historical and artistic interest, a true museum 'palace, still full of life'»[19].]

With the exception of a few tile panels in the Galeria dos Reis, which seem to be of Spanish origin, and others of Dutch origin in the Sala dos Painéis, the rest are all Portuguese.

[To this date it has been impossible to discover where they were made, not only because the construction of the Palace] took some years but also because, not counting the rest of the country, «there were thirteen tile factories in Lisbon during the early seventeenth century, as well as twenty-eight kilns for Venetian china»[20].

In the Iberian peninsula it was the Arab domination which introduced us to tiling, but its origin seems to have been the Orient, where the Persians learned the technique which in turn was transmitted to the West.

Portugal went through a period of prosperity during the sixteenth century and in consequence of this there was an artistic boom resulting in the restoration of many palatial buildings, manors and churches.

But it was in the seventeenth century that tile work achieved its highest point of recognition with the famous panels in which European and Oriental cultural elements intermingle and, later, figures representing memorable events. Both are collections of rare and monumental beauty.

The figurative panels show profane representations, such as those found near the entrance to the Casa de Fresco and on the façade of the

Above, detail of one the panels of Dutch tiles in the Sala dos Painéis. It portrays a battle between Centaurs and the Lapithae.

In the Sala das Batalhas a tile panel showing the Batalha das Linhas de Elvas. A panel shows a mounted knight, the Count of Cantanhede, commander of the Portuguese troops.

Palace, as well as the characteristic collection of horsemen shown in the Galeria dos Reis and the allegorical panels on the chapel's terrace, in addition to scenes in more secluded spots, such as the «macacarias».

This monumental use of tiling on the exterior of the Palace finds its counterpart in its interiors, of which most are horizontal. A beautiful example is the Dutch one in the Sala dos Painéis.

«It was not without difficulty that the Dutch products entered our country... Complaints and requests for protection were made and in 1687 the Conselho da Fazenda decided to proclaim protectionist measures. The edict was sent to the Provedor da Alfândega de Lisboa stipulating that tiles coming from outside the kingdom should not be cleared by the customs... The same Royal Council decided to raise the embargo on the importing of tiling in 1698, thus leaving the coast clear to all those coming from Holland».

Details of stucco work in a corner of the Sala das Batalhas with a figure playing a song of victory on a trumpet.

Converted to the blue and white of Chinese china, Portuguese tiling, in its prime, acquired a superior quality of which magnificent examples can be seen in the Sala das Batalhas, with interesting representations of the various battles fought during the Wars of Restoration.

A great tile painter, António de Oliveira Bernardes, [later] contributed decisively to this revival of the national tile work. He founded a school for ceramic artists, who kept up the high standard of this «minor art» until the end of the eighteenth century.

It was Dom João II who gave the impulse to the Portuguese arts, hiring foreign artists which led to «the appearance of a transitional style, called Manueline, during the next reign»[21]. From this time on, our country was visited by artists of various nationalities, particularly Italians, whose influence in Portugal is felt to this day. A few «years before the earthquake of 1755, a gifted Italian artist, João Grossi, came to Lisbon and started works of this kind. Another stucco artist, Gommassa, at first a mere assistant to Grossi, became famous... With the earthquake, fast work became necessary and the stucco workers prospered; there were others too, such as Cantaforo and Agostinho de Quadri... The Marquis of Pombal even founded a school for stucco work, with Grossi as the teacher (1766)»[22].

II

The Palace has two very distinct sections: «part of the interior decoration which is of the eighteenth century, and the exterior with its extremely rich ceramic decoration of the terraces and gardens, dating to the original Palace. This makes it the most interesting and complete example we have of a seventeenth-century manor house»[23].

It was built by the Count of Torre and first Marquis of Fronteira, Dom João de Mascarenhas (1632-1681), who built it on «the Mascarenhas' lands, partly acquired by him, called Morgado Novo»[24]. «Twenty-six thousand Reis were paid for a quinta which they call Lourejos and which is next to the Convent of São Domingos de Benfica. It is a noble's quinta». Thus says the inventory made on the death of the first Marchioness of Fronteira, Dona Madalena de Castro.

In spite of the Marquise's having a large income, the construction of this Palace absorbed it all, and the Marquis of Fronteira hesitated as to whether or not he should «keep the Quinta at Benfica founded by his father, or mortgage other assets to pay for it». For according to the inventory, his father owed his eldest son nearly five «contos» from his mother's inheritance and had incurred many other debts. It is curious that the sale of the quinta should have been considered, because «selling the Palace for more or less everyone would have gained or lost, and damages to the Marquis of Fronteira would not have been so high»[25].

A view of the garden from the (south tower) Torrinha Sul towards the tank and the Galeria dos Reis.

Cosimo de Medici, Grand Duke of Tuscany, in his official account of his voyage through Spain and Portugal[26], concluded that the beginning of construction dated prior to 1669. On 7th February 1669, an entry in his diary reads: «Il dopo desinare fu a S. Domenico di Benefica a veder la Villa del Conte della Torre...».

There is a footnote transcribing part of Corsini's account referring to the visit, in which someone from the Prince's retinue said: «questa (villa) si va al presente fabbricando con galanteria é picoletta, et ha contiguo un giardino, con diversi perterri, statue e bassirilievi, ma assai ordinarj, vi sono cinque fontane grandi, et altre piccole in varie altezze distribuite per l'ineguaglianza del sito; vi é un laghetto, et un Laberinto serrato di spalliere di limoni e due grotte ornate di madreperle, pezzi di porcellane, vetri di diversi colori, e scagliette di marmi, di più sorti, che for mano all'occhio una vaga, e ben concertata prospettiva.

La casa tutta, con le muraglie del Giardino é ornata di maioliche figurate, rappresentanti diversi historie, e favole, dicono, che fino ad ora vi habbi speso detto signore 50 000 cruzadi, e vi resta ancòra molto da fare».

From this description, the oldest known, one can infer that the gardens were already completed by that time even though the Palace was still under construction and a long way to completion.

Dom Pedro II conferred the title upon the Marquis of Fronteira on 7th January 1670, which explains why Cosimo de Medicis, who visited the Palace on 7th February 1669, mentioned the title of Count of Torre.

More detailed information is given to us in the «Inventory and will made on the death of Donna Magdalena de Castro, Marchioness of Fronteira», who died on 10th September 1673[27], and in a book written by Alexis Collotes de Jantillet, *Horoe Subsecivoe*.

This book is dedicated to the son of the founder of the Palace, third Count of Torre and second Marquis of Fronteira, Dom Fernão Mascarenhas and, from pages 106 to 119, describes the Palace in the following manner:

On a bench outside the Casa do Fresco a tile panel shows two musicians playing.

«*Villam sive Pretorium Marchionis Fronterioe Bemficanum (eruditissime vir) suadeo ut videas, ego nuperrime vidi, non sine poenitentia tarditatis; atque ut tibi cupiditatem illuc eundi injiciam, lubet pulchritudinem et gratiam loci describere, quantumque memoria, et cogitatione in species rerum defixa assequar, oculis tuis subjicere*»[28].

In the same vein, this interesting description continues:

«I advise you to see the Marquis of Fronteira's (a most learned gentleman) country manor or Palace of Benfica which I visited a few days ago, feeling very sorry for having taken so long to do so; you will most certainly want to go there, when you have read my description of the beauty and charm of the quinta.

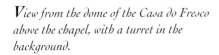

View from the dome of the Casa do Fresco above the chapel, with a turret in the background.

«I have no doubt that larger ones can be found in any part of Europe, particularly if you consider that it does not yet have the amplitude and disposition marked out on the plans; but it is not only the size that favors the house, but also the amenity of the gardens unblemished all year round, because the moderate summer and winter weathers keep the trees and flowers in a perennial leafy greenness.

«This country house lies a mile from the city, in a place they call Benfica, from whence its name comes; entering through the north side we first go through the court, then two porticos, one of which has a triple arcade, with six golden columns on each arch supporting the vault; the next one also has six arches and columns in bluish Alentejo stone. After the porticos one comes to an elegant court where the two wings join; here are two small fountains on the walls supporting two sylvan medium-size heads in marble spouting water. Farther on, a portico gives access to several entrances; passing through the medium arch, the visitors come across a crystal clear fountain and in it a sylvan head piping water into a shell of pure white stone; the fountain is decorated with two dolphins whose tails are raised to the sylvan figure and their mouths, eager for water, reach towards the shell.

«On the right and left of the fountain are two flights of marble stairs opposite to each other to reach the upper story. They have a series of straight steps which then curve when arriving at the upper story where small square statues in marble face each other. The stair railings display columns supporting porphyry globes. These stairs lead into an ample

Detail of a winged cupid in stucco above the main entrance to the Palace.

One of a series of painted panels in the Sala dos Painéis showing a battle between the navies of Portugal and the Netherlands. Set below the moulding, each of the panels is framed with a symmetrical stucco moulding, a device typical of late Baroque, early rococo decorative style.

and cheerful room, which the visitor enters through a door on the left which takes him to a portico of three arches and six columns followed by another equal in arches and columns, both overlooking the court.

«I could call this upper portico, with a pleasant view of gardens and fields, a conservatory, a shelter from the cold winter storms. It keeps out the harsh north winds and preserves the heat of the daily sun; at the end there are two small luxurious chambers. Outside, underneath the windows, are two stone statues gushing water into a lake which runs along the whole building.

«Following the last of the small chambers one comes to a large room decorated with beautiful statues and cymas. The walls are lined with expertly painted panels and the lower part of these are encrusted with a white background of tiling which is painted in a bluish color portraying battles the Portuguese fought against the Spaniards.

«The view from three windows is of an enclosed path abounding in perfumed jasmine and gentle niches tapering off at the top and interlaced in relief, from the midst of which flows a spring out of a serpent's gaping mouth.

«In the large room a two-sided entrance opens onto a delicate path; its pavement is remarkable for its multicolored stones. On the right there is a wall and on top of it are arched cupboards displaying images of the liberal arts, perfectly painted, on joined bricks; semicircular niches dug between the cupboards include seven alabaster figures of planets referring to gods, one of which is Apollo; nearby there are excellent statues of Marsyas, stripped of his skin; at their feet, several figures

A tile panel set beneath a flower box on the chapel terrace. In the panel, a monkey drives a horse-driven chariot at a gallop.

expel water through pipes which falls in a soft murmur onto the fake shells overlaying a small paving where it is absorbed by lead holes.

«Circular walls resplendent with various kinds of flowers and fruits decorating the highest parts and the gaps are decorated with men's busts. On the opposite side along the length of the path, there is a beautiful marble gallery, containing vases with flowers and benches for the weary visitors.

«At the end stands a private chapel, the construction of which is magnificent. The vestibule, which has not been completed, is lined with glazed mosaics representing various figures; to those arriving a winged child offers water flowing from a bronze jug onto a stone sculpted into little shells.

«Leaving this path there are three entrances with three double-sided doors. One leads to a dining hall with wood paneling, painted very white, with large mirrors, woodcarving and Italian stone embellished by wooden flowers; following this one is another, equal to it in the abundance and richness of ornate furniture, which has inlaid work of tortoise shell and gold; the lower parts of the walls are surrounded on the sides by imported paintings from Holland[29], imitating varied kinds of paintings of game, hills and woods. There is a secluded chamber in this dining hall, decorated with a mixture of gold painting and where one could sleep on the small cots and couches provided; other chambers and recesses follow which were used as the servants' quarters when the family came to live in the country.

«To reach the lower part of the Palace one descends a marble staircase; this part is allotted to the rural workers and servants, but even so, few rooms can compete with them in elegance and decoration, particularly the oblong dining hall, next to the path, which is embellished with little flowers of subtle painting scattered on the ceiling in a haphazard and cheerful manner; on the walls hang different kinds of mirrors with frames of tortoise-shell, ebony and other precious materials, decorated with gold and silver engravings.

«From here we pass through a low portico to the greenhouse. After passing over a small bridge on the lake, looking towards the upper part of the garden the view is of sixteen large plots of land, each one cut out in flower beds of a million shapes, hemmed in by trimmed myrtle, exhibiting a variety of multicolored flowers. A display of statues of men and women standing on pedestals completes the garden's magnificent decoration. It is irrigated by five fountains built with remarkable skill and laid out in a checked pattern: here water springs from a white lily and there, water spouts into the air through many tubes from a vase of the purest crystal.

«The space between the first path and the fountains is noteworthy for its magnificent stature: Four crowned putti facing each other are placed at the top of the marble columns. These eject water through

Terrace view of the chapel with open door. Opposite page, a bench in the Jardim Grande in tile with an image of children at play. Most likely, this was copied from an earlier tile panel in the nineteenth century.

trumpets into a large porphyry basin; leaning against them is a large circular vase, supported by a sphere, which is in turn upheld by another vase, in jasper, encircled by golden heads of satyrs also gushing water. The insignia of the owners of the Palace are depicted on the globe and around them are many sonorous tubes.

«The garden tapers off into a shady corner. Take a minute to wander off towards a vault supported by four columns and shaded by thick grapevines; underneath stands an enormous solid stone porphyry table, with small seats round it; here the gigantic trees keep the strong winds away during the Winter and in the Summer offer the shade of their thick branches to those who pass.

«Nearby is another lake, long and rather wide where it joins the garden. There you will see a little golden boat and ducklings swimming. In each of the four corners of the lake a statue leans on the marble balusters impetuously throwing water into the air which falls into the lake making a rather pleasant noise. Both sides of the lake have marble railings on top of which vases full of flowers and figures of nymphs are placed at equal intervals.

«On the other side, delineated in arches and columns, is a higher wall on which the ancestors of the Mascarenhas family and the most distinguished are painted on horseback wearing breastplates which fill in the spaces between the columns. On the lower part of the wall there are three grottoes: the middle one shows Mount Helicon with Apollo and the Muses and Pegasus kicking the top of the mountain with his hoof; water runs from a fountain in the other two grottoes.

«Bordering each end of the tank are two similar sets of stairs with banisters and statues in resplendent marble, with two interesting towers at the top. On either side Mercury is depicted wearing a hat, raised wings and caduceus. Perched on the tip of his left foot, he stretches the other leg as if about to fly off.

«A path stretches between the towers overlooking the tank, and borders the wall which has railings decorated with a long row of statues; an opening in the middle railings shows the figure of Mercury standing on a golden sphere; on the remaining railings there are various niches containing elegant work in glazed tiling with busts in onyx of the Lusitanian kings.

«One of the towers admits us to a portico decorated with many statues and from there a few more steps lead to a small and cheerful terrace.

«This terrace is paved with square stones and shaded by trees; here we find a small wall on which a skillful artist has depicted the Mascarenhas' coat of arms; a pelican and its young along with other birds. The wall also features inlaid work of various forms and colors.

«The tank is contiguous to the terrace and in it one can see a flock of beautiful swans swimming; the edges are enclosed by statues pouring water through multiform tubes.

The figure of an owl in tile at the entrance to the Galeria dos Reis.

«From here one descends to a wood through sinuous footpaths that double back on themselves in a labyrinthine way; here one finds a shady place woven with leafy little green branches arched over four elegant columns; a pyramid made from glass fragments and china; a kind of ornament covered with big and little shells and pearls. Water is expelled in the shape of an open crown; nearby there is a couch where you can lie down if, on a Summer's afternoon, you feel like taking a nap to the sound of water falling slowly in the background.

«A small nursery garden can be found next to the labyrinth and at the top of it a small refectory with three distinct compartments, beautifully lined with glazed tiling, containing three statues and the same number of fountains.

«Facing the refectory is a small lake lined with white tiling; in it are four copper globes shooting water into the air through four narrow holes, and two dolphins in fountains, with naked little boys in marble sitting and blowing on their backs. Surrounding the lake and bordered by thick boxwood are two flower beds planted with narcissi, daisies, hyacinths, tulips, bluebottles, anemones and other garden delights. The fountain of Venus occupies the space between the flower beds. The goddess is made from polished marble; crushing her breasts, she throws water into a rounded shell below. This shell is supported by three dolphins whose tails are knotted together and their heads are placed on three turtles which also pour water into a large basin. From the nursery garden we turn to the lower quarters of the Palace by passing through a rounded doorway.

«Next to the Palace is a kitchen garden and at the top of it is a military road leading to Lisbon. In the middle, a discreet plot of land on a wooded hill welcomes those arriving. A tank to which three fountains lead feeds these trees; the first emanates from an eagle's head and the water coming from it looks like a sheet.

«From the top of the hill one descends to a large plain which is rich in all kinds of horticultural goods, be they local or foreign. In the center is a vast octagonal receptacle with a dolphin at each corner pouring water from its mouth. In the center lies a block of marble surrounded by four fountains which spout from the heads of four animals. Another, slightly smaller, receptacle stands on the block and beneath it, a little shell on a jasper stay which a maiden crushes with her feet. She carries in her hand a tube, from which many pipes throw water which splashes together with an agreeable murmur.

«In addition to a higher exterior wall, an interior one surrounds the garden. It is lower and separated alternately by flower beds and benches. A vast plain follows with apple trees planted in straight rows.

«Several orchards and vineyards still surround the country house and in the middle of these there is a hill covered with roses, the beauty of which is unbelievable. Nearby there is a lovely group of fertile hills and fields. From here the group of buildings can be seen with the Convent of the Order of S. Domingos predominating.

«All of this contributes to the pleasure of those who pass through, as well as to those lucky enough to live here.

«The things I have described to you, you will be able to see for yourself, should you be able to take the time off from your affairs. That is, unless you cannot tear yourself away from your beloved city and do not wish to see them.

«Good-bye. Lisbon, 11th April 1678.»

Alexis Collotes de Jantillet said all this when talking of his visit to this quinta «which I visited a few days ago feeling sorry for having taken so long to do so». These words prove that the building was already considered an interesting architectural complex at the time.

It is believed that the Palace was inaugurated with «a picnic given in honor of King Pedro II»[30] followed by a hunt, and that the *Companhia das Indias* china used for the banquet was purposely broken, so that nobody else could use it again. With the broken bits, bizarre patterns were made to embellish the fountains, grottoes and pavilions.

However, during these nine years (1669-1678), an event took place which helps place the date of inauguration. Dona Madalena de Castro, wife of the Marquis, died on 10th September 1673. Therefore «it is not likely that the Palace would have been inaugurated in such a pompous manner during the following years»[31].

Due to this, and because peace with Spain only came about in 1668, the Marquis, then Count of Torre, was on the battlefields before this. We can therefore surmise that «the new Marquis might have inaugurated his Palace in 1671 or 1672»[32].

It has been seen that this first Palace, or country house, according to Collotes de Jantillet, or hunting lodge, as tradition has it, was the foundation for the present one. From the above-quoted descriptions it can be deduced that, although not as complete as it is today, it was already splendid.

Tradition has it that the primitive Palace was situated in the Terreiro do Trigo, where to this day the ruins of «a seventeenth-century portal and a fortified corner adorned with the Mascarenhas' arms»[33] can be seen.

This was confirmed in the inventory made on the death of the first Marchioness of Fronteira. A document was annexed to it, dated 1652, which referred to the Countess of Torre, Dona Maria de Noronha, widow, living there.

The Palace was inherited by the Count of Conculim, third son of the Marquis of Fronteira, who suffered greatly from the 1755 earthquake. But «already on 19th November 1724 a terrible gale, after having destroyed the Santarém quay, washed much water from the Tagus river

Plate inscribed with the arms of the Mascarenhas family. Manufactured in the nineteenth-century, this set was called 'Palais Royal' and might have been brought back to Portugal when Dom José Trazimundo Mascarenhas returned from exile in France.

and stones from the quay into the house of the Counts of Conculim»[34].

Ramalho Ortigão says, quite rightly[35], that nothing remains of the Palace where the Marquises of Fronteira lived. It was «in the Chagas zone, between Rua das Chagas and two others, Rua da Emenda and Horta Seca. Marquis Dom Fernando withdrew to the Benfica quinta after his house had been completely destroyed by the 1755 earthquake and died shortly after»[36].

What is a fact is that it was the great earthquake which gave the incentive to enlarge the primitive country house, or hunting lodge, into a house of residence. Only after that did the Fronteira family move to Benfica[37].

The earthquake of 1755 was terrible and one can say that «it was an unfortunate period of our history. The great genius of the Marquis of Pombal erased practically all signs of it»[38]. But what he did not manage to do was recuperate the valuables lost in the cataclysm, for which Lisbon, as the capital city of a rich empire, was an important repository.

[With the Mascarenhas family scattered all over the world, fighting the infidels and spreading the Faith, the losses at the Fronteira Palace were inestimable.]

As an example of what was lost, the inventory made on the death of the Marchioness of Fronteira refers to eighty-six tapestries, «excluding those hanging between the windows, over windows, over doorways, wall coverings and bed covers, the number of which was not always mentioned, as well as numerous carpets... This must have been a remarkable collection not only for its calculated value but for its size»[39].

The whereabouts of these materials, comprising «one of the most complete documental collections of its kind», are now unknown, and it is believed that they were most probably lost in the earthquake.

According to the same inventory, the first Marquis of Fronteira commissioned artists from Flanders: Piter Clangen Heyn, Albert Auwerce and Guilliam Van Leefdael, to make a great number of these tapestries.

It was the first Marquis of Fronteira, and sixth Count of Torre, Dom José Mascarenhas, who inherited the house from his brother, Dom Fernando, and who did not leave any heirs, who enlarged and made some improvements to the primitive lodge.

It is an interesting coincidence that the eleventh Count of Torre, tenth Marquis of Fronteira, eighth Marquis of Alorna, twelfth Count of Assumar and Conculim, also Dom José Mascarenhas, also made great improvements which were imperative there[40], as without them we would, sooner or later, have lost another bit of our national heritage.

It should be brought to notice that the first chapel is dated 1584, as can be seen on a tablet placed above the doorway. This leads us to believe that other buildings must have existed on that site.

To quote the words of Gabriel Pereira, «it is a pity not to know the formation of this house well, because it is remarkably preserved, a rare example in Portugal»[41].

A porcelain vessel for tea with a cannister hung beneath the vessel's spout. It is assumed to have been manufactured toward the close of the Ming Dynasty (1368 - 1644) and would be classified as Chinese Export Porcelain made expressly for the European market. The vessel might have been used for serving coffee after it was brought to Portugal .

The Palace

«Built in the style fashionable in Italy at that time»[(42)], the Palace gives from its exterior no idea of the beautiful and interesting interiors it contains.

Ramalho Ortigão says, «the pavilion and the Galeria dos Reis are the work of an Italian artist whose name I cannot recall»[(43)]. He goes on to say «the general outline of the two terraces in loggias over a vast lake in the Italian Renaissance style, has a glaring likeness to the Villa Madonna in Rome, work of Julio Romano and Rafael, today in ruins»[(44)].

[According to some people, the façade, of good and erudite architecture, is thought to have been inspired by a well-known design by Sebastiano Serlio. This is likely because of the popularity in Portugal of

The north façade of the Palace was recently restored and is its principal entrance. The courtyard in front was designed to accomodate twenty carriages.
Many of the Palace's architectural references can be ascribed to the Italian architect, Sebastiano Serlio, (1475 - 1554). He is best known for his "Five Books on Architecture, " as they were called when they first appeared in England in 1611. "L'Architettura e Prospettiva di Sebastiono Serlio, Bolognese." First published between 1537 and 1575. Opposite page, a pair of fountains with gargoyles flank the entrance to the Palace.

this great author of treatises. In George Kubler's opinion[45], however, the inspiration came from a painting of Villa Saúlio by Rubens.]

There are three main façades of the Palace to be considered, each one as imposing as the other but all different in design and decoration.

The one on the West side looks onto an enormous patio with two fountains. One enters this through an imposing gate flanked by railings with interesting square pavilions topped by a mythological figure at each end.

Upon entering this patio [«with room enough for twenty horses and carriages»[46]] one sees [to the right] two great wings of the Palace, built in the eighteenth century. These are adorned at midpoint with the Mascarenhas' coat of arms in stone [three golden bands on a red background] and topped by the Marquis's crown[47]. We ascend to the first landing or hall by two steps communicating with the patio, from which it is separated by eight marble columns forming three large arches.

This hall has a beautiful seventeenth-century tile panel, and on the ceiling the Mascarenhas' coat of arms are depicted in color. At the farthest end are two small flights of steps with balustrades in Carrara marble. These are finished off with four spheres of the same marble, which lead to the second landing.

This landing is reached by passing through another gate of the same style as the one at the entrance to the patio, placed here in January 1933 by the eleventh Count of Torre, tenth Marquis of Fronteira.

Following pages, just as the loggia above displays Serlian motifs, so too does the entrance to the Palace with its three arches and square openings above them. The entrance steps in marble were placed there by the eleventh Count of Torre. At the right is a sculpture by Pedro Fazenda from the collection of contemporary art collected by the Fundação das Casas de Fronteira e Alorna. The principal entrance to the Palace. Faced with tiles in a camellia pattern, it has a marble fountain at the center with dolphins and a gargoyle representing Neptune.

On both sides of this gate on the first landing one can see two hollowed out stones «which were used for extinguishing the torches which lit the way for the cars and carriages»[48].

On the second landing, used as an entrance hall, there is a big stone arch trimming a niche lined with beautiful azulejos «with a figurehead at the farthest end which comes out of a shell supported by two dolphins; water gushes into a lovely basin, all in Carrara marble»[49].

Leading to a third landing in two symmetrical flights is another stairway with banisters in Carrara marble topped by eight spheres in rose-colored marble. It has a beautiful wainscotting of azulejos and on the 10.42 meter high painted ceiling one can see a colored medallion representing Jupiter, which is sublime.

The upper floor of the main entrance with a portrait of the seventh Marchioness of Fronteira The typanum above the one of the doors are the arms of the Távora. Following page, the wall of the entrance hall. Sponged to make the wall resemble marble, a false window is also included in trompe l'oeil.

There are five doors on this landing: three lead to the Sala das Batalhas, one to the Sala dos Painéis, and the other to a lovely gallery in Italian style.

Of the three doors in front leading to the Sala das Batalhas, the middle one has the Marquises of Fronteira's and Counts of Torres' arms above it. On either side of this door are two interesting oil portraits [representing two ladies attempting to take their own lives]. Above the side doors hang two gold embroidered silk standards showing the arms of the Marquises of Távora.

[This Palace contains rooms of great artistic and historical value as well as several communicating annexes which were altered making it impossible to determine the phases of their development accurately.]

A rococo candlelabrum in gilded bronze. It stands on a bracket made in Empire style.

The Sala das Batalhas. One of the tile panels. Here, the Battle of Ambixiel is portrayed, showing the Portuguese and Spanish troops engaged in battle.

SALA DAS BATALHAS

This is the grandest and most striking of all the rooms. It has three windows overlooking the Jardim de Vénus, and seven doors. The Sala was thus called because the original azulejo paneling represents the main episodes of the Wars of Restoration.

Eight paintings fill a third of the lower part of the walls. These refer in chronological order to the following battles:

Battle of Montijo — 26th May, 1644
Combat of Arronches — 8th November, 1653
Battle of S. Miguel [Seige of Badajoz] — 22nd July, 1658
Battle of the Elvas Lines — 14th January, 1659
Battle of Ameixial — 8th July, 1663
Battle of Castelo Rodrigo — 7th July, 1664
Battle of Montes Claros — 17th July, 1665
Skirmish of Chaves — 20th November, 1667

These panels, undoubtedly made in Portugal, possibly by a combatant or an observer, have a great many interesting details portrayed in them. A small description of the most important of these is engraved on the tiles themselves, as well as the names of the Portuguese and Spanish generals who distinguished themselves most in those battles. These are reproduced below in the same order as the battles:

Primeira erigurroza batalha q' ganharão asarmas portuguezas aordem doconde deAlegrete noscampos deMontijo depois desehaverem redemido doiugo Castelhano ditozo evenerado auspicio da futura gloria dePortugal cuio espetaculo solemnizou afama com sustentar ocampo egozar de todos osdespoios emsinal da victoria triumphante de 4000 in-imigos entre mortos eferidos q' com oseu sangue rubricarão pa sempre Amen gloria aosvencedores

Terrivel efuriozo combate deArronches emq' contendendo cavalaria com cavalaria gan-harão asinvenciveis armas portuguezas amaior gloria vencendo etriunfando domaior numero semq'lhepudesse rezistir aventage de 1200 cavalos comq' osCastelhanos se oppunhão a 800 cavalos portuguezes sendo general dacavalaria nesta ocasião Andre deAlbuquerque desaudosa elevvavel memoria q' soube esmaltar nest dia q' se contarão 8 de Novembro de 653 asua fama com oseu sangue tão generozamente vingado q' lherendeo avida oconde deAlmarante oprimeiro cabo das tropas deCastella comperda de 400 soldados e de 900 cavalos q' se tomarão vivos e fi-carão mortos nocampo

Vigoroza ardente efortada batalha de S Miguel expugnação eescalada do mesmo forte notavel emaior exemplar dovalor portuguez q' contenidendo entre tres ataques pelejavão pella frente com o exercito Castelhano sendo batido do forte eda cidade pella retaguarda epello costado conseguio aretirada do inimigo quelhe deixou ocampo eorendimento do forte

An inscription on one of the tile panels "Ospurtuna máxima, sempre assaz gloriosa Batalha da Linhas de Elvas, 14 de Janeiro 1659." In the tile appears the second Conde da Torre who is battling a horse and then dismounting the horse's rider.
Detail of the encircled town of Badajoz with the Spanish lines of defence and the River Guadiana. The Spanish wear green plumes in their helmets and on their canon also green; yellow represents the Spanish flag.

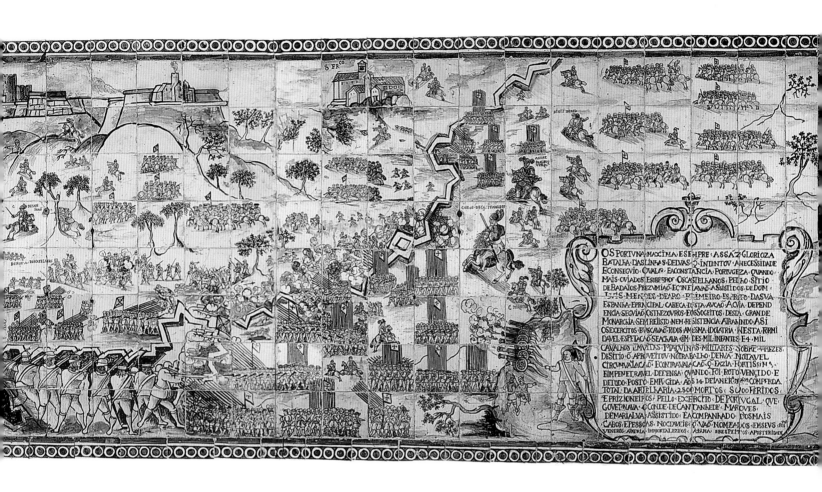

OS PORTVNA MAXIMA E SEMPRE ASSAZ GLORIOZA
BATALHA DAS LINHAS DE ELVAS Q INTENTOV A NECESSIDADE
E CONSEGVIO OVALO E A CONSTANCIA PORTVGEZA QVANDO
MAIS OVIADOS ESCOBEROS OS CASTELHANOS PELLO SITIO
DE BADAIOS PREZVMIAÕ E CÕ NELA VAÕ ASSISTIDOS DE DOM
LVIS MENDES DE ARO PRIMEIRO ES PRITO DAS VA
ESPANA E PRINCIPAL CABEÇA DESTA AVCAÕ A CVIA DEPEND
ENCIA SEGVIAÕ OS TREZOVROS E OS SOGEITOS DESTA GRANDE
MONARCHIA SEM RELISTO NEM RESISTENCIA ATRAHINDO ASI
OS EXERCITOS BVSCAVAÕ TODOS A MESMA IDOLATRIA NESTA FORMI
DAVEL ESPETAC O SE ACHAVA CM DES MIL INFANTES E 4 MIL
CAVALHOS E MVITAS MAQVINAS MILLITARES SOBRE A TEZES
DE SITIO O APROVEITOV NO TRABALLO DE NVA NOTAVEL
CIRCVNVALACAÕ E CONTRAVALACAÕ Q FAZIA FORTISSIMA
E IMPENETRAVEL DEFENSA QVANDO FOI ROTO VENCIDO E
DETODO POSTO EM VGIDA AOS 14 DE IANER CÕ COMPERDA
TOTAL DA ARTELHARIA 2500 MORTOS SU oo FERIDOS
E PRIZIONEIPOS PELLO EXCERCITO DE PORTVGAL QVE
GOVERNAVA O CONDE DE CANTANHEDE MAROVES
DE MARIALVA ASSISTIDO E ACOMPANHADO DOS MAIS
CABOS E PESSOAS NOCIAVEIS O VAÕ NOMEADOS EM SEVS
VENEROS E APERIA IMMORTALEZEOS ABAHA E RESPEITOS A POSTERIDADE

CIRCVNVALCAÕ DO INIMIGO

GAV DIANA

DE S XPTVAÕ

q' lhe coroou avitoria immortaliando afama de ioane Mendes deuas conselhos q' governava as armas sera eterno onome dos que oa judarão elhe assistirão neste combate que seconseguiu a 22 de Julho de 1658 dedicado immutavelmente asmemorias da Magdalena

Os fortuna maxima esempre assaz glorioza batalha das Linhas Delvas q' intentou anecessidade econseguio ovalor eaconstancia portugueza quando mais oviados esoberbos osCastelhanos pello sitio de Badaios prezumião econfiavão assistidos de Dom Luiz Mendes Dearo primeiro espirito dasua Espanha eprincipal cabeça desta aução acuia dependencia seguião ostrezouros eossogeitos desta grande monarchia sem registo nem resistencia atraindo asi osexercitos buscavão todos amesma idolatria nesta formidavel espetação seachava com des mil infantes e 4 mil cavalhos emuitas maquinas militares sobre mezes desitio q' aproveitou notrabalho dehua notavel circumvalação econtravalação q' fazia fortissima e impenetravel defensa quando foi roto vencido e detodo posto emfugida ãos 14 dejaneiro de 1659 comperda total daartelharia 2500 mortos 5000 feridos e prizioneiros pello exercito de Portugal que governava oconde de Cantanhede Marquez deMarialva assistido eacompanhado dosmais cabos epessoas noctaveis q' vão nomeados emseus postos veneros apatria immortalezeos afama erespeitos aposterideda

Altissimo enseaimaimportante memoravel batalha Domigial q' ganharão asenvensiveis armas portuguezas asitidas da direcção do Conde Devillaflor eosmais cabos e pessoas notaveis...... em seus postos aonumeroso vetereno easis formidavel exercito deCastela que governava Dom ião de Austria oprimeiro Castelhano que por suas virtudes fama nasimento heomais natural filho de Felippe 4 idisputada econseguida aos 8 deiunho de 663 com total rota detodo oexercito eperda universal do trem bagagens eartelharia demais de 3000 mortos e 4000 feridos e 6000 prizioneiros sobre muitos cabos officiais epessoas degrande conta egrandes deespanha edous mil cavallos q' se tomarão vivos fora osmortos eferidos que ficarão no campo

Ditoza e preciza batalha deCastelo Rodrigo q' sendo sitiado pello Duque deOsuna em 7 deiulho de 1664 em q' asarmas doreino seachavão divertidas com Dom ião deAustria nos empregos de Alenteio aconseguio oval or eaindustria dePedro iaques de Magallhes oppondosse aoexto deCastela com orespeito do nome portuguez q' empoucos paizanos do partido deriba coa foi tao terivel que bastou pera dezaloiar oinimigo com avista primeiro q' com osmosquetes metido emretirada lhe largou oposto esendo seguido até orio Agueda aventage dositio lhefes voltar acara eesperar formado donde foi roto com total perda doexto artelharia ebagagens sem q' daparte dos portuguezes ouvesse mais q' um soldado morto

Felice contigente eimproviza batalha dos Montes Claros q' na primeira marcha do exercito de Portugal q' sahio em socorro da praça de Vila Viçoza governado pello Marquez de Marialva foi acometido pello de Castella a ordem do Marquez de Caracena q' com ardente e vigurozo impulso pode romper o corno esquerdo até a retaguarda donde foi rebatido tão rigurozamente q' acabou em fugida o q' comessou em vitoria e foi roto comperda total do exercito Castelhano deterna gloria dos portuguezes comperda de 3000 cavalos e seis mil infantes entre mortos e prizioneiros e preza de toda a sua artelharia ultimo e memoravel combate entre as duas coroas

Sala das Batalhas. A stucco equestrian portrait representing
Dom João de Mascarenhas, second count of Torre and builder of
the Palace of Fronteira.

Ultimo egenerozo combate dacavallaria q' conseguirão asarmas portuguezas naprovincia Detras-Osmontes aordem doconde de S. ião Marquez de Tavora q com ardente efelicissimo espirito superou com oseu valor ecom asua industria as ventages dos Castelhanos podendo triunfar domaior numero conseguio esta vitoria compresa de 300 cavallos eroína total detodas astropas inimigas em 20 de Novembro de 1667

The figures have extraordinary movement, giving the illusion of distance, «the Portuguese attacking or awaiting, in battle line, the battle orders; the Spaniards fleeing in a disorderly fashion, in difficult and ridiculous positions...»[50].

In addition to the inscriptions just referred to, which are enclosed in a small frame, one can detect others scattered throughout the picture, surmounting figures which speak of battle sights: Elvas, Badajoz, Vila Viçosa, Estremoz, etc., as well as of several fighters such as the Count of Torre, Marquis of Távora, Dom Pedro de Almeida, Count of Amarante, Duke of Cadaval, Count of Mesquitela, Count of Vila Flor, Count of Cantanhede, Baron of Alvito, Dom João da Silva, Sergeant-Major Dom

Tapestry manufactured at the end of the seventeenth century with the Mascarenhas arms at the center. At the top is the crown of the Marquis. Then in what can only be described as watch hands, is of the seal of different Portuguese families: Manoel, Lobo, Athaide and Sá. In the central part of the tapestry other Portuguese families are also recorded:Silva, Menezes, Almeida, Silveira, Sousa, Costa, Noronha, Castro, Mendoza, Câmara de Lobos, Carvalhosa Pallhavã and Lima.
Opposite page, detail of a stucco portrait of the Conde de Conculim. On the right, a bust in stucco of Dom José Luís Mascarenhas, fifth Marquis of Fronteira.
Below, a curious detail of a stucco figure.

Stucco work in the Sala das Batalhas showing the delicate articulation between the walls and ceiling design. The asymmetry of rococo ornament is evident in the stucco detail, accentuated by the use of gold-leaf, another typical rococo design element.

Filipe Roxo, André de Albuquerque, etc. The enemies are included too: Dom João de Austria, and with more prominence, Don Luís Mendes de Haro, Duke of S. Germain, Duke of Luna, Duke of Ossuna, Don Gaspar of Lacueva, Marquis of Caracena, Don Vitor Tarragona, etc.

Alexis Collotes de Jantillet had already mentioned the Benfica tiling in his work, and Luís Teixeira of Sampaio refers to the dining hall's «unequaled historical value»[51].

These panels should be considered unique both as ceramics and from the historical point of view. José Queirós describes them in the following way: «A 1.66 meter high blue and wine color tile panel. Within a small ornate border, several battles of Restoration, the Count of Torre having fought in some of them. War topics are not isolated compositions, they are scattered about in groups containing foot soldiers and horsemen, and, in several places, fortresses and castles... Some carry inscriptions relating the details of decisive battles; others, indicating the places where the most important combats were fought and the names of the gentlemen who led them»[52].

[Santos Simões makes the following remark: «As an historical document and iconographic testimony, this Galeria das Batalhas will be one of the most valuable works of tiling made in Portugal; it is a pity that it was not signed, as the artist would have gone down in history, not so much for the excellence of his art work, but certainly for his picturesque interpretation»[53].]

This room which has already been used as a dining hall and a ballroom [today it is used for most of the cultural activities of the Foundation of the Casas of Fronteira and Alorna], measures 11.5 meters in length by 9 meters in width and 7.12 meters in height. Its decoration is pure eighteenth century[54].

Above the tile panel representing the Battle of Ameixial, with the «founder of the house locked in physical combat with the Castilian General, Dom João de Austria»[55], «the life-size portrait of the first Marquis of Fronteira on horseback wearing Marshal's uniform»[56] stands out «in high relief» bearing the following inscription:

DOM JOÃO MASCAR[AS] I[O] MARQVEZ DE FRONTEIRA = 2[O] CONDE DA TORRE: S.[OR] DA V.[A] DE FRON-[TRA]COM[DOR] DO ROSMANINHAL E DE OVTRAS 5. COMENDAS NA ORDEM DE CHRISTO: NA GVERRA DA RESTAVRAÇÃO DESTE REINO M[RE] DE CAMPO GEN.[AL] DO EXER-CITO. E PROV.[A] DO MINHO. M.[RE] DE CAMPO GEN.[AL] E GEN.[AL] DA CAVELARIA DA PROV[A] DE ALEMTEJO. M[RE] DE CAMPO CENT[AL] JVTO À PESSOA DE EL REI NA CORTE, E PROV[A] DA ESTREMADVRA. E GOVERNADOR DAS ARMAS DE CASCAES. E SETVBAL: GEMTIL-HOMEM DA CAMERA DE EL REI D. P.[O] 2[O], SENDO PRINCIPE REGENTE: DO SEV CONS.[O] DE ESTADO. E GVERRA: VE-DOR DA FAZENDA E PRIOR DO GRATO DEPOI,[S] CONTA VA POV-COS DIAS, QVÃDO O SORPRENDEO A MORTE, CHEIO DE GLORIA MILITAR, E POLITICA, EGREGIAM.[TE] ADQVIRIDA, NA GVERRA PELLO SEV MARCIAL ESFORÇO, E PROVIDA CON-DUCTA, COMQ FOI GRANDE PARTE NAS MEMORAVEIS VICTORIAS. DAQVELLE TEMPO; E NA PAZ PELLA SVA INTELIGENCIA, CIRCVNSPECÇÃO, E ACTIVID.[E] NO EXERCICIO DOS SEVS SVBLIMES EMPREGOS, EMQ SE MOSTROV DIGNO DE TODOS: VALEROZO, PRVDENTE, E MAGNIFICO, DO QVE NÃO HE O MENOR MONVMENTO ESTA QVINTA QVE

FVNDOV, E EXORNOV COMPLETAM;ᵀᴱ BENEMERITO DOS SEVˢ PRINCIPES, E DA PATRIA, E GLORIOZO A MEMORIA DOS SEVS DESCENDENTES ENTROV NA SVA ETERNIDADE EM 16 DE SETTEBRO DE 441681=48 ANNOS 12 MEZES. MENOS 2. DIAS.

The effigies of four celebrated Mascarenhas are depicted in relief in the central portion of the ceiling: Dom Francisco, Dom Filipe, Dom António and Dom Gil Anes. On the walls above the doors and windows are more members of the family with the following inscriptions, also in low relief:

*I*n a corner of the Sala das Batalhas, a medallion in stucco with a bust of Dom Filipe Mascarenhas.

Dom Fernão Martins Mascarenhas

Senhor de Lavre, Comendador de Mertola, e de Almodovar: Alcaide Mór de Monte Mór o Novo, e de Alcaçar do Sal: Capitão dos Ginetes dos Reis D. João II, e D. Manuel: Chefe dos Mascarenhas.

Dom Manuel Mascarenhas

Do Cons.o de El Rei D. João III: Com.dor do Rosmaninhal: Filho do 1o Capitão dos Ginetes=Foi na tomada de Azamor em 1515; e depois famozo Govern.or de Arzilla, onde morreu em Set.bro de 1545: chamado pelas suas façanhas=o da espada cortadora.

Dom Fernando Mascarenhas

Do Conselho de El Rei D. Sebastião, Comendador do Rosman.al. servio com seu Pai em Africa, e depois por m.tas vezes; onde, acopanhando ao d.o Rei, foi morto na bat.a de Alcacere em 4 de Agosto de 1578=Inst.or do Morgado da Torre, em Julho de 1572 annos.

Dom Manuel Mascarenhas

Do Cons.o de El Rei: Comend.or do Rosmaninhal: servio em Africa com seu Pai=Foi mal ferido e cativo na bat.a de Alcacere, e depois Govern.or de Mazagão=Falleceo em 5 de Março de 1612.

Dom Fernando Mascarenhas

1.o Conde da Torre: do Cons.o de Estado, e de Guerra: Com.dor do Rosm.al, Fonte Arcada, e Carrazedo: Prezid.te do Senado: Gov.dor de Ceuta e de Tangere, Gen.al da Armada de Portugal e Castella, com o Governo de mar e terra do Estado do Brasil, E.a Morreu em 9 de Ag.to de 1651. Viveu 64 annos.

Dom Fernando Mascarenhas

2.o Marquez de Fronteira, 3.o Conde da Torre: S.or de Fronteira: Comen.dor do Rosman.al e de outras com.das do Cons.o de Estado, e Guerra: Presidente do Desĕmb.o do Paço: Mordomo-mór da Rainha D. M.na de Austria: Vedor da Fazĕda: Gov.dor do R.no do Algarve: Na guerra do seu tempo: Gov.dor das Armas da Prov.a da Beira, e das do Alemtejo: Hum dos 4 prim.ros censores da Acad.a Real da Hist.a E.a Falleceo em 25 de Fev.ro de 1729. Viveo 73 anos, 2 mezes e 11 dias.

Dom João José Mascarenhas

3.o Marquez de Fronteira: 4.o Conde da Torre: Senhor de Fronteira: Comēn.dor das Comendas de N. S.ra do Rosm.al, S. Tiago de Fonte Arcada, S. Nicoláo de Carrazedo, S.ta Christina de Afife, S. Miguel de Linhares e S. Tiago de Torres Vedras, todas na Ordem de Christo. Falleceu em 13 de Abril de 1737.

Dom Fernando Mascarenhas

4.o Marquez de Fronteira: S.or da mesma Villa: Comendador do Rosmaninhal e das outras comendas, que teve seu Pai: Veador da Casa da Rainha D. Mariana de Borbon: Deputado da Junta dos Tres Estados, E.a Falleceu em 14 de Agosto de 1765: viveo 48 anos menos 2 dias.

Dom José Luis Mascarenhas
5.o Marquez de Fronteira.

Dom Francisco Mascarenhas

1.o Conde de Coculim: S.or de Coculim e Verodá no Estado da India: Comend.dor das Comendas de S.Martinho de Cambres. S. João de Castellã, S. Martinho de Pina, na Ordem de Christo, E.a Filho 2.o do 1.o Marquez de Fronteira.

As I have already stated, it was the fifth Marquis of Fronteira, Dom José Mascarenhas who enlarged and improved the Palace, and to confirm my opinion, the above inscriptions referring to him are restricted to his name and title with no other reference. There can be no other explanation for such concise inscriptions about someone who would have had so much to tell.

[Worthy of notice is the carpet depicting Mashad, the capital of Horasan, in Northeastern Persia, in the second half of the nineteenth century, copied from a model and representing the Garden of Paradise.]

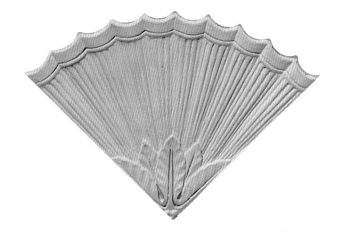

LIBRARY

This oblong room, or gallery, communicates with the stair landing and is finished off at each end by a square turret.

The turret on the right has a beautiful skirting of original blue tile work; there is a vaulted ceiling, [and paintings] and stuccoes in relief on the walls as well. The two doors and four windows are topped by medallions painted with pastoral, country, and maritime scenes. In the turret to the left there is a vaulted ceiling in faint colors with paintings of landscapes, and a skirting in monochrome tiles features copies of earlier ones.

This gallery has lovely paneling in modern tiles[57], with an interesting frieze above from the same period and a vaulted ceiling, in subdued colors, whose restoration was ordered by the first Count of Torre. [The walls are now lined with shelves, as it is currently used as the Library.]

One of the most beautiful views of the Jardim Grande can be had from this Library. It is Italian in style and bordered by a large lake with its Galeria dos Reis forming a unique ensemble.

[It is decorated with furniture dating to various periods and origins, of

In the library a detail of the bookshelves with an autographed portrait of King Carlos. In the background, a nineteenth-century Ehrard harp with a tuning fork.

which the following are particularly noteworthy: two seventeenth-century convent tables, two desks, four Empire armchairs, four ebony (Chippendale) chairs, four high-backed chairs, a Dom José cradle, two English globes (one terrestrial, the other celestial) dating to the late eighteenth century, and an eighteenth-century harp. There is also a French Ehrard piano from the last century adorned with small portraits, some with dedications of the royal family. These include Dom Luís, Dona Maria Pia, Dom Carlos, Dona Amélia, Prince Luís Filipe, Dom Manuel, Dona Filipa and Dom Duarte.]

[Also worthy of notice is a marble bust of the seventh Marquis of Fronteira, fifth Marquis of Alorna, Dom José Trazimundo Mascarenhas Barreto, who left interesting *Memórias* , published in five volumes.]

The earthquake of 1755 must have destroyed the Library of the Marquises of Fronteira, for only this can explain the lack of manuscripts, which one would ordinarily expect such an important family to possess.

[Twice during the life of the seventh Marquis of Fronteira, Dom José Trazimundo Mascarenhas, there was great confusion in the Palace, and it is likely that the books got lost when taken from their places on these occasions.

The first such occurrence took place in 1810, when Massena's army was approaching the Torres Vedras lines. Lisbon was panic-stricken, as it was feared the French would break the lines, and pillage the city. Everybody tried to hide their valuables, including those who lived in the Palace. In the rush, the hiding places were poorly disguised.

The Palace did not avoid being burgled the second time, in 1833, when Dom Miguel's troops lay siege to Lisbon. Part of the furniture was sent to Lisbon and the other to the palace in front. This palace had once belonged to Gerard Devisme and the Marquises of Abrantes, and was at that time the residence of the Infanta Isabel Maria.

Meanwhile, the Palace of the Marquis of Fronteira was invaded by a group of soldiers loyal to Dom Miguel, along with neighbors from the Benfica road and the Monsanto hills.

As Gabriel Pereira[58] reports, «This S. Domingos de Benfica must have been a curious place during the long political crisis in the first decades of the last century, because the Fronteiras and the Mascarenhas participated in the «Tentativa» of 1805 (an attempt to put Junot on the throne), and continued Liberals to the last; those of the house of Abrantes and the Dominicans were inclined to be Absolutists.»]

Despite these losses, the contents are more than enough to enrich any library and its manuscripts are considered to be of extreme value.

«The books found in the Palace must have had various origins. As the initials in some of them indicate»[59], many were brought from the house of Alorna when it was joined to the house of Fronteira.

About five thousand volumes are distributed haphazardly, and unfortunately are not catalogued. Editions of the seventeenth and eighteenth centuries predominate, as well as Spanish and Portuguese literature.

A celestial globe by the instrument maker William Cary (1759-1825).
From their shop on Fleet Street, the Cary family exported a variety of scientific instruments from London to several European countries including Portugal. The university at Coimbra bought many of the Cary instruments.

Opposite page, an overview of the library. The design of the ceiling is decidedly neo-classic in its ornament. It is considered to have been constructed during the final phase of the redecoration of the Palace undertaken by the fifth Marquis of Fronteira.

This library «contains mainly Greek and Latin classics, biographies of saints and other personages, books on geography, history, astronomy, natural sciences, military history; the whole collection vouches for the religious, learned and courageous spirit of the men of this illustrious family»[60].

Works by the Spanish authors such as Calderon de la Barca, Francisco de Quevedo, Frei Benito Feyjoo, Juan de Mena, Luiz de Gongora, etc., are to be found there, as well as works by authors of other countries: *Francicis Petrarchae... opera quae estant*, Basileia, 1544; *Opera Caecilli Cypriani Carthaginiensis Espiscopi*, Antuerpiae, 1568; *Corpus Byzantinae Historiae*, Parisiis, 1645 and 1663 ; *Historia Ecclesiastica de España*, by Don Francisco de Padilla, Malaga, 1605; *Cronica del Orden de Cister* and *Instituto de San Bernardo*, by Frey Bernabe de ..., Madrid, 1602; *Historia de la Fondacion y Discurso de la Provincia de Santiago de Mexico de la Orden de Predicadores*, by Maestro Fray Augustin Davila Padilla. Second edition in Bruxelles, 1625; *Nobiliario Genealogico de los Reys y Titules de España*, by Alonso Lopez de haro, Madrid, 1622; *Antiguedad de la muy antigua villa de Madrid*, by Geronimo de Quintana, Madrid, 1629; *Obras de la S. Madre Tereza de Jesus*, Anvers, 1661; *Espelho de Penitentes* and *Chronica de Santa Maria de Arrabida*, by Frei António da Piedade, Lisboa, 1728; *Historia de S. Domingos, particular do Reyno, e conquistas de Portugal*, by Frei Luís de Sousa, Lisboa, 1767; *Historia Genealógica da Casa Real Portuguesa*, by Dom António Caetano de Sousa, etc.

Amongst the manuscripts, I would like to make special mention of *Relações de Pero de Alcáçova Carneiro* and *Registo da Casa da Índia*, «which were considered unique in the precious and obscure collection of the Dukes of Cadaval»[61]; some chronicles of kings of Portugal from the sixteenth and seventeenth centuries such as two of Dom Afonso Henriques, one written by Duarte Galvão and the other by Rui de Pina; one of Dom Pedro I; one of Dom Fernando by Rui de Pina and two of Dom João II, one written by Rui de Pina and the other by Damião de Góis, dated 1567. There are many and varied volumes containing copies of letters and other papers. These include many letters of Filipe III written to Dom Fernando Mascarenhas, Count of Torre, the Governor of Tangiers, and to the Duke de Medina Sidónia; various letters from the Duchess of Mântua and Miguel de Vasconcelos; several from Father António Vieira; from the Marquis of Fronteira, Dom Fernando de Mascarenhas, Governor of the Province of Alentejo; letters from ministers and other individuals, correspondence of André de Melo e Castro, appointed Count of Galvêas, Ambassador to Rome, to the Count of Assumar, from 1719 to 1728; correspondence from Father António do Rego, Portugal's resident in Rome, to the Count of Assumar, Portuguese Ambassador and Carlos III, from 1705 to 1708; correspondence from the Count of Atalaia, commander of the Portuguese army in Catalunha, to the Count of Assumar, Portuguese ambassador to His Holy Catholic Highness from 1705 to 1714; correspondence from the Count of Tarouca, Portugal's Plenipotentiary to the Hague, to the Count of Assumar, from 1720 to 1727; correspondence from Francisco de Sousa

Pacheco, Portugal's envoy to Holland, to the Count of Assumar, Portugal's Ambassador to Carlos III, since 1695 to 1704; letters from the Count of Vila Verde to the Count of Assumar, Portugal's special Ambassador to Carlos III from 1706 to 1713; collections of copies of letters to His Majesty's ministers and other individuals, written by the Count of Assumar, His Majesty, the King of Portugal's special Ambassador, to King Carlos III, in Barcelona in 1708; several collections of copies of letters and official letters to Count of Oyenhausen; several volumes with the title *Various and curious papers* where the most varied matters are discussed, many of interest to historians; three thick volumes of the *Tombo da Comenda* by Salvador de Baldreu; all of Alcipe's manuscripts, a few of them unpublished; correspondence from the Count of Torre, Dom Fernando Mascarenhas, Governor of Ceuta and Tangiers, who died in 1651; two or three hundred letters from the second Marquis of Alorna, Dom João de Almeida Portugal, written from the Junqueira prison to his wife, unpublished and essential to the clarification of a few of the obscure points in the Tavora family history. Also in the collection are many and varied letters dating to the beginning of this century from members of this family and which shed much light on many of our country's historical events.

TORRINHA SUL

Adjacent to the library is the south tower. Its tower room is a chamber with box-like proportions: narrow in width, it rises to a domed ceiling, creating a vertical space. The dome, with its exuberant figures in stucco set against a painted backdrop, is perhaps the epitome of rococo style at the Palace.

The lower portion of the chamber's walls are covered with blue and white tile in what has been described as a seventeenth century pattern.

Torrinha Sul, detail of the ceiling.

Above the tiling and the dado-rail, the stucco ornamentation rises in a herbaceous motif, to the domed ceiling above. In the central part of the dome painting and stucco work are articulated in delicate colors and clouds which lend a transparent, almost skylit, effect. Presiding over the dome is a goddess; identified by some as Pallas Athene, she is more likely to be Demeter because of the child and the wild animal that accompany her. Surrounding the goddess are four *putti* with garlands of flowers and motifs in stucco representing the earth and sky. These images in turn are dominated by their respective spheres.

The paintings on the upper portions of the walls of the chamber are seasonal landscapes in pre-romantic setting.

The stucco motifs of Earth and Sky placed against a painted background.
On the right, a painting at the base of the dome, representing a scene with ruins, typical of the period.
Opposite page, an overall view of the domed ceiling.

GALLERY

This room, which is similar to the previous one, has monochrome tile paneling and looks onto the entrance patio. It must have been the original dining hall as it is decorated with colored fruits on the ceiling and the walls. [It was later used as the Billiard Room for quite some time, having been turned into the Library by the eleventh Count of Torre.

[The gallery was recently reopened, with three verandahs facing the patio.] These are decorated with a gray-colored marble arch which is

In the gallery hangs a portrait of Dom Francisco de Almeida, first Viceroy of India. Below, a fawn figure with the countenance of a gargoyle and worked in stucco.
Opposite page, a mural painting in fresco of a large bird cage <volière> with perching birds, creepers and other plants in blossom.

View of the gallery. Above the doors are fanlights in trompe l'oeil with gargoyle figures in stucco and garlands above them. At the center is a rustic and polychromed press-cupboard of Portuguese manufacture dating to the seventeenth century.
Above, an Indo-Portuguese seventeenth century accounting desk in pyramid shape.

supported by marble columns of the same color, making a total of eight columns and three arches.

Opposite to these verandahs are three others with marble balustrades overlooking the great entrance stairway which is also illuminated by them. From any one of these verandahs the magnificence of this seigniorial entrance can be richly appreciated.

[A rustic painted cupboard exists in this gallery. It is Portuguese and dates from the seventeenth century.]

SALA DOS PAINÉIS

This new room [the present Dining Room] rivals both the Sala das Batalhas and the main bedroom in beauty, and is as grand as each of them if not more.

A 1.71 meter-high wainscoting in Dutch tiling has already been mentioned by Alexis Collotes de Jantillet. Comprising «the oldest example of tiles made in Holland for marketing abroad», [they are currently believed to be the work of Adriaen and Jan Van Oort[62], though Santos Simões attributes them to Van der Kloet.] Representing a variety of scenes, they are only one of the many intriguing works to be admired in this room.

[The mythological, rural and hunting scenes represented in these panels include «hunting the wolf (to the East), a rural scene (to the West), a ship, a fight between Zeus and the drunken Centaurs, cattle and Laphites (to the North), Pan and the transformation of the nymph Siringe into a pipe, and Demeter in her carriage pulled by winged snakes (to the South)». These works have nothing much in common, from which we can presume that the buyer limited himself to giving the size of the panels required and left the choice to his supplier.]

[There is also] a 6.65 meter high vaulted ceiling. Over each of its seven doors [one of which is false], are interesting medallions with oil paintings alternating with designs in stucco relief.

Sala dos Painéis. Detail of a panel of Dutch manufacture; in white and blue, the scene depicted on the panel is a wolf hunt.

Sala dos Painéis. The panels in this room are of Dutch manufacture and are attributed to Wülliam Van Der Kloet. In this panel the chariot of the Goddess Demeter is pulled by winged dragons. Van Der Kloet appears to have furnished the Palace of Fronteira the tiles in 1670, while the palace was still under construction. It would have taken place eight years before the Portuguese Crown restricted the import of Dutch-manufactured tiles. Below, a detail of the previous panel.

A violin in a frame moulded of stucco and above it, a bird; on either side are cornucopia with flowers.

Opposite page, the Sala is now the dining room of the Palace. The table center piece, in Empire style, is a work by Pierre-Philippe Thomire (1751-1843), the outstanding Empire Fondeur-Doreur of France. The porcelain is signed by Vista Alegre, a Portuguese manufacturer. In the background is a portrait of the second Marchioness of Alorna, dressed as Diana, the huntress. Beneath is one of the Dutch-manufactured tiles that face the lower portion of the room's walls.

Below, a press-cupboard of the seventeenth-century. The exterior of the cupboard is decorated in Chinese style with lacquer and gold-embossed landscapes set on a green background. Inside, the same landscapes are repeated, this time with a red background.

In this room there is a beautiful gold carved oriental table with a marble top worthy of a museum, two gold painted «trumeaux», [and a seventeenth-century Indo-Portuguese cupboard imitating Chinese laqueur. This last contains a French dinner set (Palais Royal) with the family's arms on it.]

The following paintings can be seen hanging on the walls: [three, of the second Marchioness of Alorna, executed in Belém; two, of the second

A detail of the ceiling ornament. The painting is framed in stucco with a herbaceous borders. At left, a candlestick in rococo style and an ink well with the arms of Almeida Portugal. The pieces are thought to have been brought to Portugal by the Marquis of Alorna upon the terminaton of his services as Portuguese Viceroy in India. The ink well is said to have been used by the Viceroy's niece, Leonor de Almeida Portugal, known as Alcipe, a member of an Arcadian group of Portuguese poets. Opposite page, Sala dos Painéis. paintings representing maritime scenes, framed in stucco with herbaceous motifs, cornucopias and baskets of flowers.

Marquis of Alorna, in one of which he is dressed in a Louis XV costume; one of the first Marquis of Castelo Novo and second Count of Assumar, as a reward for his military exploits while Viceroy in India (1744-1750); one of the sixth Countess of Ribeira, daughter of the Marquises of Alorna; one of the Countess of Serzedas, and another of a relative of hers.]

Paintings of ruins in the Sala dos Painéis. Opposite page, the central motif in the ceiling - a gilded lyre, in stucco and crowned with a radiant sun.

Sala de Juno. A medallion representing Music set in an ornament of Empire style. Below, a miniature eighteenth century commode. Behind it, a skirting board of Dutch tile and dating to the seventeenth- century. Below left, a small table in Louis XV style for needlework. According to the Mascarenhas family, it was given to Alcipe by Marie Antoinette, Queen of France.
Opposite page, a view of the Sala de Juno. At the eastern end of the room is a fireplace of English design in marble and green coloring. Most likely it was manufactured at the close of the eighteenth century. Above the fireplace hangs a portrait of Dom Carlos, Dona Leonor and Dom José Trazimundo Mascarenhas Barreto. The painting is attributed to Domingos Antônio de Sequeira (1768 - 1837).

SALA DE JUNO OR SALA IMPÉRIO

This Sala Império, is also known as the Sala de Juno, as this mythological figure is the central subject on the vaulted ceiling, which also shows beautiful painted medallions in *mesofresco* on stucco in relief.

Over the fireplace hangs a large painting by Domingos Sequeira or Pellegrini, representing the three young brothers: Dom José Trazimundo, seventh Marquis of Fronteira, Dona Leonor Mascarenhas, wife of the Count of Alva and Dom Carlos Mascarenhas.

[Also of importance is a pastel drawing of Alcipe, as a young girl, and an oil painting of her in old age[63], another of Dona Henriqueta de Oeynhausen e Almeida, Alcipe's daughter, and yet another of Alcipe's mother, and her grandmother, the Marchioness of Távora.

Occupying this room are two beautiful Louis XV chests of drawers, a miniature writing desk of the seventeenth century, a miniature eighteenth-century chest of drawers, and a Spanish leather screen from the same period. Several pieces of rare and beautiful Saxon, Chinese and Japanese china are scattered about the room, including a «Companie des Indes» ink pot featuring the Almeida Portugal crest which belonged to Alcipe.]

*S*ala de Juno. On the south wall of the room is a detail of a tempera painting of a flower vase flanked by two griffons.

SALA DOS QUATRO ELEMENTOS

This small chamber has a lovely skirting of Dutch tiling in blue and a vaulted ceiling with oil paintings and stuccoes. In the midst of this ceiling, stucco work featuring the four elements is depicted surrounded by a circular element with vegetable motifs.

Of the furniture, we would like to point out a beautiful English Grandfather clock, an interesting Indo-Portuguese cabinet «contador» in the very unusual shape of a pyramid, and two other, smaller «contadores». All three date to the seventeenth century.

On the wall hangs a large portrait signed by Pellegrini[64], featuring the famous general, the third Marquis of Alorna[65], Dom Pedro, Alcipe's brother, his wife, and their two children who died very young.

[Another painting shows the fifth Marquis, Dom José Luís Mascarenhas.] There are also two large portraits of the seventh Marquises of Fronteira [Dom José Trazimundo Mascarenhas and his wife, Dona Constância da Câmara], painted in Rome by Silvagni.

[Two small portraits of the Spanish School of Painting, presumed to be of Dom Lopo de Almeida and his wife, Dona Joana de Portugal, founders of the Almeida Portugal family, can also be found in this room. These date to the turn of the sixteenth century.]

[Also noteworthy are the poetical works of the (Alcipe)], which can be found here in six volumes, richly bound in velvet and gold.

The Sala dos Quatros Elementos. Two of four paintings of landscapes inserted in the glass doors that separate the Sala de Juno from the Sala dos Quatros Elementos.

Sala de Fumo, also called the Sala de Quatro Estações. The painting framed in stucco is unique for its large proportions.
Below, Sala de Aparato. The room dates to the eighteenth-century and the painting is ascribed to Pedro Alexandrino and shows Mars courting Venus. On the right, Eros secures the shield of Mars.

SALA DE EROS

Formerly the Sala Cor-de-Rosa, this room has stucco work on the ceiling representing Eros, or Cupid, blindfolded with his bow and arrows.

On the walls are several panels of tile work dating from the second half of the eighteenth century. Depicting elegant scenes in blue, they are encompassed by polychrome tablets with inscriptions.

According to the Marquis of Ávila e Bolama, this was Alcipe's room when she stayed at the Palace.

SALA DAS QUATRO ESTAÇÕES OR SALA DE FUMO

This sala, actually two rooms with low ceilings has, in each of them, marvelous wainscoting of different [Pombaline pattern] tiling. On the walls of one of the rooms are paintings on stucco depicting pastoral, fishing and hunting scenes.

THE BEDROOM

The construction of the bedroom, which can be seen to the right upon entering the patio, dates from the time of the fifth Marquis of Fronteira, Dom José Mascarenhas. The [murals] «painted by Pedro Alexandrino»[66] are admirable, the ones on the ceiling being more recent[67] than those along the walls.

Amongst those on the ceiling there is a large panel depicting Venus, Mars and Hephaestos, while above the two doors and seven windows [oil] paintings represent various other mythological scenes and figures.

A magnificent French chandelier in bronze hangs from the marvelous vaulted ceiling. On the tile wainscoting are pictures depicting scenes of hunts. The horsemen with their lances ready to attack and their attendant packs of dogs make a surprising ensemble.

With regard to the furniture there is a beautiful Louis XVI desk, a Louis XIV chest of drawers and two low chests dating to the late seventeen-hundreds, as well as a French clock, a lovely mirror in gold carving and a magnificent eighteenth-century Aubusson carpet.

*T*he Sala de Aparato. A painting by Pedro Alexandrino showing Venus, Mars and Vulcan. In the
painting Vulcan is shown making arms for Mars who stands by contemplating Venus. The
painting is set in a stucco frame with garlands of flowers considered rococo in style. To the sides
are frames with medallions at the center, suggesting a early neo-classic style. Below the painting
is a panel of tiles from the second half of the eighteenth-century representing a stag hunt.
To the right, detail of one of the medallions.

Sala de Aparato. A painting representing Astronomy.

THE TERRACE OUTSIDE THE CHAPEL

Overlooking the Jardim de Vénus, this terrace with its five communicating doors to the Sala das Batalhas and Sala dos Painéis is one of the most suggestive rooms of the Palace.

At the upper end there is a porch supported by four marble columns. There are three doors here: the middle one has a small step leading to the chapel; the one on the right is a private entrance to the Palace; and the left one leads to a [small] staircase with a vaulted ceiling, completely covered in beautiful [monochromatic] tiling. This last door leads to the Jardim de Vénus, or the Jardim de Cima.

On leaving the Sala dos Painéis, one sees over one of the doors «two

Terrace leading to the chapel, on the tympanum above the narthex is a ceramic medallion of the della Robbia school.
Sculpture of Venus in Italian marble.
To the right, the last sculpture on the terrace represents Diana.
Each figure along the Terrace has a medallion of a Roman Emperor placed above them.
These busts were restored by Rocha Correia at the beginning of the twentieth-century.

An azulejo panel to the side of the entrance to the chapel; beyond the panel is the garden. Opposite page, terrace of the chapel. This is the Gallery of Art, the Promenade of the Oratoria, ending at the entrance to the chapel., showing elements in ceramic from the della Robbia School.

*"Astronomy." Panel from the seventeenth-century representing the Liberal Arts.
At right, an angel with bat wings.
Below, a seventeenth-century panel with two side benches.*

medallions portraying the first and second Counts of Torre, probably dating to the origin»[68].

The enormous terrace has small clearings bordered by a marble balustrade and flanked by small benches lined with seventeenth-century tiling. Forming a series of small verandahs, it is a real dream.

«The façade of the chapel, and of the Palace which it adjoins, are decorated in borders and garlands of fruits, foliage and flowers in high relief and strong colors, which contributed to the renown of the great della Robbia artists»[69].

Ramalho Ortigão described these decorations in the following manner: «The medallions and the vaulted arches are sublimely edged with foliage and fruits to the liking of Luca della Robbia or of the artistic representative of that immortal family in the Peninsula, the great Nicolo Francesco Pizano...»[70].

This verandah has nine niches, each one with a marble statue in nat-

Gallery of Art, detail of a panel showing oriental influence.
Below, a sphinx , detail from the panel "Rhetoric".
Opposite page, a panel with a musical scene at the entrance to the chapel.

ural size. Depicted on the Eastern wall is Apollo «and also the shepherd, Marsyas, who was skinned for having dared to rival Apollo in flute playing»[71]. On the northwestern wall are Saturn, Mars, Jupiter, Apollo, Venus, Mercury and Diana. At the base of each statue is a marble shell with a jet of water and above, medallions representing different Roman emperors. Between these niches are great panels of seventeenth-century tiles, symbolizing [in feminine figures the Liberal Arts (Astronomy, Geometry, Rhetoric, Dialectic, Music, Arithmetic and «at the chapel's vestibule», Grammar). The Faculties (Memory, Understanding and Will), some of the Senses (Liking and Touching) are also represented, with Poetry presiding over them all.]

Luís Teixeira de Sampaio, mentioning this tile work in his work *Os Chavões*, said: «In the Unhões house there is nothing compared to the English Twelve or to the allegorical figures on the great verandah of the Fronteira house»[72].

CHAPEL

The entrance door to the chapel, the middle one on the porch described above, has an inscription, which I have already mentioned but will repeat:

Dicatum charitati coeli
Januae MDLXXXIIII

Above this is a small niche containing an interesting [alabaster figure representing Hope.]

[The fact that the year 1584 is written there does not anticipate the construction date of the Palace in the sixteenth century, but it does make us believe that some sort of building or an isolated chapel existed on those lands.]

[The very small] chapel in the form of a «Renaissance style» cross[173], has a small and interesting sacristy on the Gospel side and on the Epistle side another chamber of the same style, this one dedicated to Nossa Senhora dos Desamparados.

At the entrance on each side of the door are two large oil paintings. The one on the right represents Saint Ursula [and the Martyrdom of the Eleven Thousand Virgins.] Painted exceptionally well, [it is attributed by Vítor Serrão to José de Avelar Rebelo]. The one on the left [Saint Michael Freeing the Souls from Purgatory] is, however, not particularly well painted.

Worthy of notice is a beautiful and rich tile panel. At the end of the arms of the cross are two altars dedicated to São Francisco Xavier and Santo António. 1771, [the date of the marriage of the fifth Marquis, who carried out the restoration works of the eighteenth century], is engraved in roman numbers on the base of the altar on the right. This is in harmony with the chapel's style and proves that restoration work was done there during that year. [There are also some beautiful images here, amongst them that of a Cingalese Jesus Christ dating to the late sixteenth-century, and another of Nossa Senhora do Rosário] attributed to Machado de Castro. There are also some richly decorated vestments.

S. Francisco Xavier is believed to have celebrated his last mass here before leaving for India. He died in Sichuan, near China, in 1552.

[The question arises, however, of how this can be explained if he left Portugal in the year 1541, forty-three years before the date engraved on the Chapel altar.

This leads us to believe «that the previous chapel must have had important remodeling done to it...»[74]. Due to the close relationship between the Mascarenhas and the first two Jesuits to have arrived in Portugal: «Recommended by Dom Pedro Mascarenhas, Portugal's envoy to the Holy See, the first two Jesuits came to the Court of Dom João III»[75].

These were the Spaniard Francisco Xavier who left for India, and the Portuguese Simão Rodrigues de Azevedo, who stayed in the court in Lisbon. In Rome, Dom Pedro Mascarenhas was on excellent terms with the «Mestre Inacio's companions»[76], as they were then known, and it was Simão Rodrigues himself who convinced him «to suggest to the King that» his fellow companions «be sent to India as missionaries»[77].]

Opposite page, a ceramic pine comb from the seventeenth-century above the fountain of Carrasquinha.

The Gardens

Italian in style, the gardens of the Fronteira Palace were always very much appreciated by foreign visitors, who have described them in all their magnificence.

There are many doors leading to the gardens, some directly from the Palace itself or the Chapel terrace, and others from the neighboring streets. Through enormous gates, one enters the Quinta[78].

Coming in through the patio door with its marvelous view, we look over an enormous open terrace with stairs leading to the Jardim Grande and flanked by a lovely Carrara marble balustrade.

This terrace carries on through a corridor which encompasses the Palace to the right, looking like a half of a frame to the two façades: to the West and South. At the end of this corridor one finds an interesting fountain with shells and whelks, chips of glass of various colors, and fragments of oriental china, all in bizarre designs. This fountain has marvelous mineral water and is known locally as the Fonte da Carranquinha.

The Eastern façade which overlays the Jardim Grande and which is similar to the main façade, has a lovely skirting in polychrome seventeenth-century tiles, «with figures and accessories alluding to Filipe IV's reign»[79].

At midpoint, this façade, has an interesting porch similar to the one at the entrance, with six marble columns and five doors leading into the Palace. The tiling in this porch depicts «hunts for wild animals, torch hunts and ox hunts, forbidden by the Kingdom's laws, Book 5, tit. 88»[80].

There are two main gardens: the Jardim Grande, Italian in style, and another smaller, more modern one, the Jardim de Vénus, which is on a higher level.

The Jardim Grande, 65.3 meters long and 57.5 meters wide, has as its background a great tank surmounted by the famous Galeria dos Reis. The Galeria boasts boxwood in geometrical and symmetrical flower beds forming streets, alleys and small squares. Twelve mythological statues and five octagonal tanks are also present. It is framed on the western side by a marble balustrade which looks over the lake of the Galeria dos Reis. To the North the balustrade passes a wall lined with polychromatic tile work representing the Four Elements (one of which is missing), the planets, and the constellations. To the South and East the walls are lined in largely blue and manganese tiles depicting the signs of the Zodiac and the months of the year. Here «fauns laugh, nymphs dance and the gods smile benevolently»[81]. All of this tile work dates to the seventeenth century.

The twelve panels just mentioned will now be described in greater detail:

Jardim Grande, partial view of the parterre with boxed hedges and a statue in lead.

JANUARY

In this picture there is an area with many trees, with ox, ploughs and men working the lands - activities characteristic of this month. To illustrate the quality of rural life, the artist has included the interior of a house, with several men and a woman seated at the fireplace, and a cat lying at their feet.

FEBRUARY

Simpler than the previous one, this panel shows several men cleaning the trees of a quinta. A house is depicted as well, and in the distance, a gentleman on horseback accompanied by his page on foot.

MARCH

Here, as in most of the pictures, rural scenes predominate: In this one, a quinta is shown, with various houses in the distance and birds in the air. Two men walk through the sowed fields; on top of a distant hill, a gentleman on horseback can be seen, and lower down, a cavalry detachment with its standard flying.

APRIL

This panel is somewhat different from the previous ones. Here flowers are dominant: a great palace is shown along with its vestibule and terrace. A balustrade frames the garden with its beautifully designed flower beds, in the midst of which is a basin with two dolphins coming out of it supporting a shell topped

with the figure of a man holding a flag which says "April". In the garden stands a man, in the company of a lady, dressed according to the period: cape, breeches, buckled shoes. A little removed from them, a man greets another lady who is leaving the palace.

MAY

This month is represented by a fortified coastal village, with a wharf where a boat has just come alongside to fetch a gentleman who is bidding farewell to a bishop. In the distance are two vessels; one is saluting the village and the other approaching the bar. Both the boat and the fort fly flags bearing the word "May". The surrounding countryside is thick with trees and birds.

JUNE

Here a flock of sheep grazing and its shepherd are the dominant figures. They are near a house where a man is getting ready to shear a sheep while a woman, holding another, prepares to milk it. An earthen pot stands next to her. In the distance a man on horseback teases a bull while another hands him banderillas. The bull, wild, charges the horseman. A board nailed to a tree indicates that it is the month of June.

JULY

Rich wheat-land predominates here, with a man in the middle of the fields holding in one hand a flag with "July" written on it and in the other an ax. There is a great abundance of rabbits and hunters, each one doing something different. One throws an arrow, two others hold a net with a rabbit caught in it and nearby one lies dead on the ground. Farther away are two other hunters with guns, shooting at partridges. There are also many trellised vines with grapes, and a rabbit is calmly eating some of those fallen to the ground.

AUGUST

Like the previous one, this tile shows rich wheat-land where several men are reaping. Next to them lies wheat that has already been reaped, while another man carries a load on his back. There is also a house with a walled quinta. On top of the wall is a boy picking grapes and passing them over to another who is below. Inside the walls are many fruit trees, and under one of them sits a man and another is lying down contemplating two birds who bring a ribbon in their beaks which reads "August". Two oxen rest beneath another tree, one of them lying down.

SEPTEMBER

Grape gathering is represented here in some of its phases: Several men carry baskets full of grapes on their backs and heads. Four of them head for the vintage tank with a woman inside it. Near a house, a monk with hat in hand gives thanks to God for the good harvest. In the other hand he holds a flag which reads "September".

Opposite page, a detail of "November" from the panels describing the months of the year. Above, Galleria dos Reis, a detail of a view. At right, bust of Dom Dinis in the Galleria dos Reis. The tiles that surround these busts are made of a reflective material of Spanish origin.

OCTOBER

Part of this panel shows a field where a yoke of oxen move with a plough harnessed to them. Farther on is a man with a flock of sheep. Another walks swiftly with a stick over his shoulder and a basket in his hand. He has a gourd lashed to his waist on which "October" is written. Elsewhere there stands an olive grove with two men up in a tree knocking down olives, which are caught in a basket by another man.

NOVEMBER

This tile shows a quinta with plenty of trees near a house. Hanging on a stick suspended from two trees is a pig that is being cut open by a man who has a tub next to him full of its entrails. Farther on, a woman looks after a fire with a pot which is hanging from a chain tied to two trees. Another man hangs a ham to smoke. There is also a man leading a herd of pigs, and who carries in his hand a flag which reads "November".

DECEMBER

A field with many trees is shown, with several boys enjoying themselves snar-

Opposite page, Galeria dos Reis, sculpture on the upper terrace by Pierre Mignard.
This illusory portico contains a restored sculpture in bronze. The busts of Dom Afonso Henriques, Dom Sancho 1 and Dom Afonso II are placed by the tower.
At right, one of the panels of azulejos above the tank representing one of the twelve knights inspired by Velasquez.

ing birds. Amongst them is a gentleman with a sword at his waist, wearing a large hat with a ribbon which says "December". In the distance another gentleman walks, and two men can be seen cutting down a tree with an ax. On another plane, a yoke of oxen pulls a plough which is driven by a farmer.

At the center of this garden, in the largest square, is one of the octagonal tanks which has at midpoint a column with four niches. In these are cupids, which form the base for a beautiful and artistic basin. From this rises another column in marble topped by an armilary sphere which has the Mascarenhas crest and the crown of a Marquis on it.

The great tank is spectacular, and serves to highlight and confirm the prestige of its adjoining garden. It and the Galeria dos Reis alone, even without Fronteira's other treasures, would serve to justify this monograph.

The rectangular tank, 50 meters long and 19 wide, has a balustrade in Carrara marble, with a majestic stairway with two flights, 3.2 meters in width, to each side. These give access to an elegant pavilion leading to the Galeria dos Reis.

[Nearly all sixteenth and seventeenth-century gardens and their intricate patterns were designed to be admired from terraces. Dom João Mascarenhas, however, outdid himself in transforming the terrace into a spacious outdoor gallery overlooking the tank that is itself an admirable architectural structure.]

At the end of the tank a high wall was built, lined by twelve tile panels with three grottoes, [all of them encrusted with pieces of glass, china, shells, pebbles, etc., in an art known as embrechados.] There are also two more panels to the sides with a fountain at the center and two beautiful statues on either side.

These «large tile panels depict handsome horsemen with feathers galloping in a proud and warlike dash, a recollection of the marvelous Velasquez equestrian paintings of Prince Baltasar Carlos, Filipe IV

Opposite page, view of the tank with a rising stair, the two sculptures represent Aurora and Lígia.

Another knight along the tank, there are several interpretations for these figures: illustrious figures of the Restoration, members of the Mascarenhas family or English knights.
Above, a triangular tile panel at the base of the stair at the Galeria dos Reis representing Neptune.

and Count-Duke of Olivares at the Museu of Madrid,,[82].

These panels are referred to both in the inventory made on the death of the first Marchioness of Fronteira and in the already-mentioned description by Alexis Collotes de Jantillet.

It says in the inventory: «...on the right side of the garden is a large lake with rounded stone railings with seven large jasper statues with thirteen white stone vases. Also this lake has three arches, each one with its own house and niches; there are fourteen arches. On the end wall is tile paneling with laurels and cornices in embrechado and monograms. Midway are figures on horseback with the Mascarenhas titles, in the middle arch a Mount Parnassus with nine jasper figures, each four palms high...».

View of the Galeria dos Reis. The two statues in the lake represent Dirce and Leimon Opposite page, a sculpture in lead in the garden.

Collotes de Jantillet carries on in the same vein. «in which the ancestors of the Mascarenhas family and the illustrious personages are portrayed on horseback, with breastplates...».

The spirit with which this house was built - these gentlemen on horseback, their clothes and bearing — confirm that these panels represent distinguished personages, amongst them the Mascarenhas who brought such celebrity to Portuguese horsemanship[83]. Two lateral panels have been identified.

The panel on the left represents Dom Fernam Martins Mascarenhas, Capitão dos Ginetes dos Reis, Dom João II and Dom Manuel, head of the Mascarenhas. All but Dom Fernam carry a Marshall's baton, while he, unlike the others, is framed by eleven medallions representing eleven members of the Mascarenhas family, with a border around him depicting the titles he gave which originated from him:

Count of Santa Cruz, Count of Óbidos, Count of Torre, Count of Conculim, Marquis of Fronteira, Marquis of Montalvão, Count of Sabugal, Count of Serém, Count of Castelo Novo, Count of Palma, Count of Vila da Horta.

All along its base the following words are written on a waving ribbon:

Titles which will flourish in this distinguished lineage

The panel on the right has no words and is provided with a border of coats of arms which correspond, even in their order, to those decorating the tapestry. These belonged to Dom Fernando Mascarenhas, second Marquis of Fronteira, who is also represented in this panel.

At the center under the Marquis's crown, are the Mascarenhas' coat of arms, replaced in the above-mentioned tile panel by a figure on horseback who while much younger than the others has the same military bearing.

We conclude that this panel on the right depicts Dom Fernando Mascarenhas, third Count of Torre and second Marquis of Fronteira, «because the coat of arms shown could only belong to him...»[84].

The Galeria dos Reis, overlooking the great tank with its beautiful Carrara marble balustrade and enormous window containing a statue of Iris, Goddess of Opportunity, ends with two elegant pavilions, to which I have already referred. These are topped by Mercury, who joins this gallery to the corresponding stairway.

There are twenty-four marble busts of the kings of Portugal in this gallery, beginning with Count Dom Henrique, father of Dom Afonso Henriques, and ending with Dom Pedro II, as Prince Regent. His crown rests at the base of the bust while the others all have their crowns on their heads.

Not counting those on top of the pavilions' doors, most of them are placed in niches «lined with curved scale like tiles, translucent red with metallic reflections, bunched together. In my opinion they were probably made in Spain»[85].

Detail of a panel at the entrance to the Palace, showing a dragon.

Amongst these busts are those of the Infante Santo (Holy Prince), Dom Nuno Álvares Pereira, Dom Fernando, and one of the Roman Emperor Tiberius, which tops one of the doors of the pavilion on the right. The three Filipes are obviously not included.

José Queirós describes this gallery in the following way: «The whole gallery is lined with tiling, with the exception of the pavilion doors and the niches which shelter the busts of kings.

The decorative bands of tile work covering the background of the three arches and the ceilings of the pavilions is exceptional. Some are imbricated, in relief with metallic golden-coppered reflections; others are pine-shaped in relief, in bunches of four and molded diagonally to the square of each tile; some are in blue, others in the same shade of the imbricated glazed tiles»[86].

From the pavilion one goes on to a new gallery with four niches which contain the royal busts of Dom João V, Dom José, Dona Maria I and Dom João VI. This gallery leads to the Jardim de Vénus with its statue of the Goddess, which is on a higher level than the Jardim Grande.

At the center of groups of ferns and camellias is an octagonal lake with three entwined dolphins, «carved from a lovely block of marble»[87]. These hold up a basin in which stands the pink marble statue of Venus. Nicolau Tolentino refers to this Venus in his *A Função* [88].

On one of the edges of this garden stands the Casa de Água, or do Fresco, preciously decorated inside and out with [«fine embrechados of

At right, detail of te Casa do Fresco showing mosaic of pieces of procelain, glass and stone fragments.
Below, a view of the Casa do Fresco, at the center two children are riding sea horses. On the frontispiece is the coat of arm of Dona Madalena de Castros, first Marchioness of Fronteira.

*I*nterior of the Casa do Fresco showing a
detail of the fountain with a fawn at the
center.
At right, detail of the S tank with fish.

*O*pposite page, a detail of a tile panel on a bench by the Casa do Fresco; below a panel with a border depicting a coral fising scene and above it, a panel of cats and monkeys representing scenes with music lesson and a barber shop.
Below, the border of a bench at the same site showing mythological figures.

Detail of an azulejo panel at the entrance to the chapel with a mermaid and a triton. Opposite page, a detail of the south façade of the Palace.

shells, fragments of oriental china, black glass, flint glass, bits of dross laid out in complicated patterns»[89], as well as with polychrome tiling from the second half of the seventeenth century. It is the most beautiful embrechado grotto in existence in Portugal, following the Italian «ro-cailles» style created by João de Udine in 1525, at Villa Madama in Rome, and in the Jules Romains Grotto at the palace in Mantua.]

At the front is an interesting lake known as the S tank. Its exterior is lined with tile work representing marine fauna, and running along it are "two semi-circular benches, also with tiling [which show different kinds

of fishing (coral, line, net, pearl)], on the lower part; on the upper part (backs of the benches), amongst arches with vegetable motifs, are allegorical figures of Music and Dance. An orchestra is made up of singing and playing cats and monkeys. One of the monkeys plays an organ; another, wearing glasses, conducts the concert, while a third, with a ferule in hand, waits attentively, ready to punish those who are out of tune...

All this tiling is polychromatic and dates to the early seventeenth century»[(90)].

On yet a higher level of this garden is a new, rectangular lake, known as the Lago dos Pretos, with nine niches and mythological figures.

[Along with the Palace and its gardens, the beautiful and luxuriant woods surrounding them are also worthy of notice. Some of the original vegetation of the Monsanto hills can still be found here, making a natural setting for this Palace.]

A nineteenth-century copy of a lost panel at the entrance to the chapel.
Opposite page, a statue in lead of a dancing musician.

The Mascarenhas Lords
and Founders of this Palace

Nobility of lineal descent is a
monument of the past.
Alexandre Herculano

The Mascarenhas family is one of the oldest, most noble and distinguished of Portugal.

Titles such as the Dukes of Aveiro, Marquises of Gouveia, Fronteira, Montalvão, Counts of Santa Cruz, Castelo Novo, Vila da Horta, Sandomil, Torre, Conculim, Alva, Palma, Sabugal and Óbidos and other estates have belonged to this family.

[Many of these titles] no longer exist, some are in the hands of other families for lack of a male heir the titles went to the female branch.

The titles of Marquises of Fronteira, Counts of Torre and Conculim still run in the Mascarenhas family, to whom the Palace of S. Domingos de Benfica belongs.

In all the branches, the Mascarenhas always distinguished themselves, and there are few families who can boast having had so many eminent men and who throughout the centuries contributed to the advancement of their country.

Those who leaf through our history will come across consecutive generations of celebrated diplomats, brilliant writers, skilfull politicians, eminent monks or friars, competent colonial administrators, fearless sailors and particularly, formidable generals. For they most distinguished themselves in the art of war.

The history of India, Brazil and all of Northern Africa cannot be written without mentioning this illustrious family; all of these places speak of the bravery of the Mascarenhas.

They were Viceroys in India[91], Governors of Ormuz and Ceylon, Governors of Brazil, Governors of Ceuta, Arzila, Mazagon, Tangiers, Azamor, etc., and there was even a Mascarenhas[92] amongst the five Governors of the Kingdom nominated by the Cardinal, King Henrique for when he died. This one was no more and no less than Dom João Mascarenhas, the famous defender of the second siege of Diu in 1546, one of the greatest military feat of all times. It became known as the Lusitanean Troy.

«The fearful siege of Diu and the great victory the Portuguese had obtained from the most powerful of Kings of all the Orient, was talked about throughout Europe...»[93]. This remarkable achievement was illustrated in one of Viceroy Dom João de Castro's tapestries (Inventory of Viena Nº 94, 3.45 metres by 5.30) depicting «the peak of the famous and tragic second siege of Diu which was upheld by the invincible bravery of their Captain, Dom João Mascarenhas...»[94]. He was counsellor to King Sebastião and when consulted about the unfortunate event, he objected strongly to it. The King was indignant and attributed the prudent counsel to Dom João's advanced years, to which he answered: «My Lord, I have eighty years with which to counsel you and twentyfive to serve and accompany you on the expedition».

Dom Pedro Mascarenhas left for India in Garcia de Noronha's fleet in 1511 and in the following year he discovered some islands which became known as the Islands of Mascarenhas[95].

Dom Pedro Mascarenhas fought with such bravery in India that the Governor, Afonso Albuquerque, embraced and kissed him on the cheek in public causing a jealous reaction amongst other nobles present. One of them, Francisco Pereira, turned to the Governor and said «Lord, thou dost concede such an honour only to Pero Mascarenhas.

All of us here who serve thee deserve the same and nobody has granted us any favours, it seems that only Pedro Mascarenhas accomplished this feat honourably, thou hast disdained all the others and this we cannot accept»[96].

In 1513 Dom Pedro Mascarenhas discovered the Reunion Islands or Bourbon and Mauricia or Island of France and in 1517 Dom Jorge Mascarenhas discovered the Lequia Islands in China[97].

One of the most important feats ever achieved by the Portuguese in India was accomplished in 1527 by Dom Pedro Mascarenhas, then Governor of Malacca, when he conquered the city of Bintam.

Whilst in Rome and as Ambassador to Carlos V, the German Emperor, Dom Pedro organized the coming of the first two Jesuits to Portugal and brought them with his Company on 17th April, 1540. His connections with the Company of Jesus were immortalized in a fresco painted by André Pozzo in the Church of Saint Ignacius, Rome. In it Saint Ignacius is seated, blessing Saint Francis Xavier who lies prostrated at his feet and Dom Pedro Mascarenhas is standing beside him.

«This fresco greatly adorns our national and diplomatic vanity, for surely there is no other foreign Ambassador portrayed in the frescos of the Churches of Rome»[98].

«In 1521 he commandeered the fleet of galleys in which the Princess Beatriz, daughter of Dom Manuel and wife of Duke Carlos, was taken to Savoy; he also accompanied Prince Luís in the expedition to Tunis in 1535»[99]. Dom Pedro became Viceroy of India at an old age and died ten months after having arriving there. His remains were later returned to Portugal where they lie in the Church of S. Francisco at Alcácer do Sal to this day[100].

Dom Fernando «was King Sebastião's Ambassador to the Council of Trento which took place in the time of Pope Pius III and where he was much honoured and held in high esteem, so much so that the Pope sent his emissary to personally acknowledge and thank him for having been so favourable towards the Apostolic Faith»[101].

Five members of the Mascarenhas family died with King Sebastião on the battlefied of Alcácer Quibir in 1578.

*P*ortrait of Dom Lopo de Almeida(?), attributed to Domenikos Theotocopoulos (known as El Greco, 1541-1641.). On Dom Lopo de Almeida's marriage to Dona Almeida de Portugal the family became known as Almeida Portugal.

***D**ona Joana de Portugal, daughter of Dom João de Portugal and Dona Madalena de Vilhena, celebrated figures in the theatre piece, "Frei Luis de Sousa" by Almeida Garrett (Spanish school, last half of the seventeenth century.)*

Dom Pedro de Almeida Portugal, third Count of Assumar, later he became the first Marquis of Castelo Novo. He was Viceroy of India.

Dona Maria de Lancastre , first Marchioness of Alorna.

Dom João de Almeida Portugal, second Marquis of Alorna . Suspected of being involved in a plot against the King Dom José I, he was imprisoned by the Marquis of Pombal. On the King's death, he was released from prison and his innocence was proclaimed.

Dona Leonor de Lorena e Távora. Following the attempted murder of the King Dom José 1, she was imprisoned in the Convent of Chelas. On the death of her brother, she inherited the representation of the Casa de Távora.

Dona Leonor Tomásia de Távora, mother of Dona Leonor de Lorena e Távora, hereditary representative of the House of Távora. She married her cousin, had two children who were sent to be executed by the order of the Marquis of Pombal.

Two portraits of Dona Leonor de Almeida Portugal, Countess of Oyenhausen. She had great influence on the introduction of pre-Romantic literary style in Portugal and in particular, she encouraged the Portuguese poet, Alexandre Herculano.

*D*om Pedro de Almeida Portugal, third Marquis of Alorna with his wife and children. He was commander of the Lusitanian Brigade of Napoleon's army and took part in Napoleon's Russian campaign. Dom Pedro died on his return from Russia in the city of Koenigsberg in 1813. His sons became the Counts of Assumar, they died without heirs. The painting is signed by Domenico Pellegrini and is dated 1805.

Dom João Mascarenhas Barreto, sixth Marquis of Fronteira. By his marriage to Dona Leonor Benedicta d'Oyenhausen e Almeida Portugal, sixth Marchioness of Fronteira, daughter of Alcipe (depicted at right), the houses of Fronteira and Alorna were joined.

Dom José Trazimundo and his wife Dona Constança Câmara, fifth Marquis of Alorna and seventh Marquis of Fronteira. Dom José Trazimundo joined his brother, in the liberal movement in Portugal's civil war. Both brothers were forced into exile and returned to Portugal many years later in the company of the third Duke of Mindelo, author of a book, "Memories of the Marquis of Fronteira and of Alorna". (The portraits were painted by Silvani of Rome.)

Don Carlos Mascarenhas, from whom descends the present representatives of the house of Marquises of Fronteira, Alorna and Tâvora.

Dona Leonor Mascarenhas, Lady-in-waiting to Queen Maria, went in 1526 at the age of twenty three to Castille with Princess Isabel's (wife of Carlos V) retinue. She was much admired by Bernardim Ribeiro and Sá de Miranda and the latter, due to her many talents, compared her to Victoria Colona[102].

She was chosen by Empress Isabel to be the future King Philip II's tutor, and he in turn was so pleased with her that he also chose her to be his son, Prince Carlos'preceptor saying: «Mi hijo queda sin madre; vos lo aveis de ser suya, tratadmele como tal»[103].

Dom Fernando Martins Mascarenhas was Grand Inquisitor of the Kingdom and Principal of the Coimbra University for eight years, a position which he «administered with great prudence and affability». He was so successful that he became Bishop of the Algarve on 5th February, 1595. He held the positions of State Advisor, Prior-mor [head of the priors]of Guimarães, Bishop of Coimbra, Archbishop of Lisbon and was one of the most important theologians of his time[104].

In 1617 whilst the Fleet for India was in Lisbon, Dom Nuno

Mascarenhas paid a visit to Dom Teodósio, father of the future King João IV, in Vila Viçosa «with the purpose of reminding him of the deadly wrong committed by the King of Castille in seizing the throne which rightly belonged to him, to which the Duke answered that the time for the Restoration of Portugal had not yet arrived»[105].

Dom Jorge Mascarenhas, Count of Castelo Novo and Marquis of Montalvão was Governor of Mazagan (1615 to 1619) when the Moroccan Civil War broke out giving him the opportunity to show the Moors what the Mascarenhas were made of. He became Captain-General of the Portuguese Armada, State Counsellor, Mayor of Lisbon, Viceroy and Captain-General of Brazil.

Dom Francisco Mascarenhas had the first orange tree brought from China to Goa which he later took to Lisbon and in 1635 planted it in his garden. «It is a pity Dom Francisco did not know the riches that this noble tree would bring to his country, he was right to have cared for it so well and he rendered a great service to Portugal, no less than the discoverers of the Orient», wrote Duarte Ribeiro de Macedo[106].

Dom António Mascarenhas «the most discontented of them all»[107] worked hardest towards the Restoration of Portugal along with Dom Antão de Almada, Dom Miguel de Almada, Pedro de Mendonça, Jorge de Melo and Francisco de Melo[108]. In the Tumults of Évora of 1637, (an anti-Philippine revolt of the people against a rise in taxes imposed by the Spanish administration then ruling Portugal), which spread to the Alentejo and the Algarve «there was no lack of people try-ing to lead them to a general insurrection which in turn would lead to the proclamation of independence»[109]. In the account, published in 1641, of what happened, it says that Dom António Mascarenhas «went to Évora to encourage the leaders and to advise them that in order to succeed they should ask the House of Bragança for support»[110].

Dom João, at the time Duke of Bragança, publicly repudiated and rebuked this revolt at that time and later on. This explains why Dom António, in the same year, 1638, assured Dom Duarte, the Duke's brother, «that there was a group of nobles determined to shake off the yoke of Castille» and begged him, for that reason[111], not to return to Germany «that in time he should concentrate all his efforts on obtaining his country's freedom and restitute the sceptre to his brother, the Duke, as was correct»[112]. All these efforts were in vain. Dom Duarte returned to Germany where he had been serving in the Imperial army and died confined in the fortress of Milan, main bastion of the Spaniards in Northern Italy.

Dom António Mascarenhas was of such a temperament that on «meeting Miguel de Vasconcelos in the cloister of São Francisco de Xabregas, passed by without raising his hat to him and when asked by nobles and monks of the Convent why he had not greeted the Secretary, he answered that he though it a kind of treason to be courteous to a man whom he was sure to kill some day»[113].

Dom Jerónimo Mascarenhas, Bishop of Segóvia, was dedicated to historical studies, having left some twenty four works, some of them manuscripts, all of them very interesting and most of them unpublished. Amongst them were: *Historia de la Ciudad de Ceuta, sus sucessos militares y politicos...* written in 1648. The original is today in the National Library of Madrid, and was published by the Academia das Ciências de Lisboa in 1915 under the direction of Afonso Dornelas[114]. Dom Jerónimo Mascarenhas went to Germany with the offices of Esmoler-Mor (Lord High Almoner) and Capelão-Mor (High Chaplain), in the retinue to fetch Queen Mariana of Austria, Filipe IV's second wife, and take her to Spain.

Dom Inácio Mascarenhas, a Jesuit priest, was one of Dom João IV's great diplomats and was chosen to go to Barcelona at the time of the Catalunha revolt, upon which the Spaniards put a price on his head. He was director of the Casa de São Roque and published an *Account of the success obtained on the expedition to Catalunha at the service of King João IV* and *Prayer exhorting the faithful and pious Christians of the Kingdom of Portugal to help their neighbours in the agony of death*[115].

Dom Fernando Mascarenhas, first Count of Torre, Governor of Ceuta and Tangiers, Land and Sea General of the Armed Forces of the Crowns of Portugal and Castille. He was the only Portuguese to have had a post in both forces during the Castillian domination of Portugal.

Dom João Mascarenhas, second Count of Torre was one of the great generals in the Wars of Restoration, governor of one of the army lines, in the battle of Montes Claros, which earned him the title of Marquis of Fronteira.

After the death of his wife he

became Prior of Crato[116] of the Order of São João de Malta and left two interesting historical works[117] entitled:

Relação das Provincias de Portugal, títulos, tribunais e rendas Reais.
Relação das coutadas e casas de campo dos Reis de Portugal.

Account of the Provinces of Portugal, titles, courts and royal revenue.
Account of the "Coutadas" and Country Manors of the Kings of Portugal.

The oldest document relating to the Mascarenhas, who are contemporaries of our first dynasty, is now in the National Archives in the book of King Dinis and his father, Dom Afonso III's enquiry into a land grant dating back to Dom Sancho I, the document is reproduced in *Monarquia Lusitana*. There are a great number of documents dating to the first dynasty relating to this family but they are all rather confusing. One thing is undeniable, that this is an old family and that «the lack of documents to prove this and the discripencies in the books on the subject should not induce us to believe that it is all an invention of the geneologists eager to give this family an antiquity that it does not have. That this name goes back to before the Avis dynasty... is an indisputable fact. The names of the first members of the family were not invented by geneologists; they exist in authentic chronicles and documents where these experts unearthed them»[118]. Very precise information is had of Martim Vaz Mascarenhas and his descendents. He lived in Évora in the reign of Dom Fernando (1367-1383) «where he owned an 'herdade'

(the same as 'quinta' but has this designation in the Alentejo region) called Enxarrama upon which the Monarch bestowed special priviledges by charter given in Santarém on 21st March of 1411 (1373)»[119].

He was the father of Fernam Martins Mascarenhas, King's Counsellor, who also lived in Évora, Lord of the 'herdades' of Enxarrama and Albacotim, this one also had special priviledges bestowed upon it by charter in Santarém by Dom Duarte on 19th July 1433[120], and who «must have been an important person and been held in very high esteem, as he held an important position in the Order of Santiago that of 'Comendador-mor' for which he had been chosen during Prince João's administration of the Order, son of Dom João I»[121].

Fernam Martins Mascarenhas had four sons: Nuno Mascarenhas, Martim Vaz Mascarenhas, João Mascarenhas and Helena Mascarenhas. I will only be referring to the eldest.

Nuno Mascarenhas, Comendador of Almodôvar, Mouguelas, Montel and Roliça and noble of the courts of Dom João II, Dom Manuel, etc., married Dona Catarina de Ataíde, daughter of Nuno Gonçalves de Ataíde who was Governor of the House of Prince Fernando and died in Fez, they had the following children: Fernam Martins Mascarenhas, João Mascarenhas, nobel of the House of the Duke of Viseu and Beja; Brites de Ataíde, who came to marry Rui G. de Azevedo, Alcaide-mor (Governor) of Alenquer and, finally, Isabel de Ataíde, who married Estêvão de Góis, Alcaide-mor (Governor) of Mértola and Counsellor to King João II.

Of these I will also only speak of the eldest, Fernam Martins Mascarenhas, Dom João II's famous Capitão-mor (mor = highest or most important) dos Ginetes[122] (a type of horse), having been his great friend of all times and the person whom he most trusted when he was Prince, and later, King. This post was of the utmost importance and trust and «was always held by men of proven merit»[123].

It is interesting that this post was maintained in the family for several generations until it became hereditory by Filipe I's charter dated 22nd March 1581, and so it went until 1676 on the death of Dom Martinho Mascarenhas, fourth Count of Santa Cruz, thus nominated in Lisbon by charter dated 6th December, 1673.

Dom Fernam was Comendador of Mértola and Almodôvar, Alcaide-mor (Governor) of Montemor-o-Novo, Alcácer do Sal and Lord of Lavre and Estefa.

He fought in the Battle of Toro beside Prince João; in 1488 he went on an expedition to Morocco where, with their Captain Fernão Martins Mascarenhas at the front «the horsemen of the guards were bathed in glory»[124], he was one of the few to witness the death of our great King João II on 25th October, 1495 in Alvor.

In the royal tournaments held in Évora in December 1490 to celebrate the marriage of Prince Afonso, who died after falling from a horse, Fernão Martins Mascarenhas was one of those who crossed lances with His Royal Highness and, as did all the others, used his motto:

Ha descubierto mi vida
Desde aqui
Gran descanço para mi

Of the post of His Royal Highness's Captain of the Ginetes on whose «prowess the welfare of the King and his kingdom depended, having always served well and loyally» we have a perfect picture in two verses from the *Porquês de Setúbal* in Resende's songbook[125]:

Porque se mostra feroz
Mascarenhas, capitão?

Why do you look so fierce
Oh captain Mascarenhas?

Dom Manuel maintained all the honours granted to Dom Fernão by his predecessor, including the post of Capitão dos Ginetes of His Royal Highness's Guards and on 8th February 1496 even granted him and his descendents the right to use the word «Dom» in front of their names and to use the square standard — a priviledge reserved for kings and royalty[126].

He was one of the few who accompanied Dom Manuel to Valência de Alcântara in October 1497 to meet Princess Isabel who he was to marry, and in March of the following year he accompanied the royal couple on the long journey they made throughout Castille. Dom Fernão married twice, his first wife was Dona Violante da Cunha, daughter of Dona Isabel da Cunha and Dom Álvaro Vaz de Almada, first Count of Abranches who died in the battle of Alfarrobeira with Prince Pedro. They had no children. This marriage was annulled on the pretext that they had too close a relationship, and in the lifetime of his first wife, he married Dona Violante Henriques, daughter of Dona Isabel Henriques and of the Governor of the Casa da Suplicação and Caudel-mor of the Kingdom, Fernão da Silveira.

Dom Fernão was buried in the Chapel in Espinheiro «under the altar steps» where there are two escutcheons bearing the coats of arms of Fernão Martins Mascarenhas on top, and beneath, those of his second wife Dona Violante Henriques. The following inscriptions are depicted bordering both coats of arms[127]:

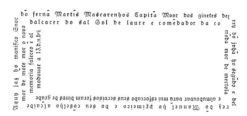

Of his second marriage, five sons and two daughters were born, all of them were entitled to use »Dom»:

1° — Dom João Mascarenhas, the eldest, Captain of the Ginetes to King Manuel and King João III, Comendador and Alcaide-mor of Mértola, Alcaide-mor of Montemor-o-Novo and of Alcácer do Sal, and King João III's Counsellor.

He stayed in Arzila until 1512 and in the following year he participated actively in the conquest of Azamor. He married Dona Margarida Coutinho, daughter of Dom Vasco Coutinho, first Count of Borba, and they had five sons and three daughters. He died in 1515.

2° — Dom Nuno Mascarenhas, was Comendador of Almodôvar and Captain of Çafim, where he became a hero. Two sons were born of his marriage to Dona Brites da Silva, daughter of João Freire de Andrade, Lord of Bobadela. He died on 31st October 1522 when he was shipwrecked of Vila Nova de Portimão. One of his sons was the famous defender of the first siege of Diu.

3° — Dom Pedro Mascarenhas, Estribeiro-Mor (Master Equerry) to Prince João and when he became King João III; tutor and Lord Chamberlain to Prince João (father of King Sebastião); Counsellor to João III and page to Queen Leonor, the King's sister. He was Capitão das Galés (Captain of the Galleys) and accompanied Princess Beatriz on them to Savoy. Ambassador to the court of Charles V of Germany and then to the court of Rome, having left Lisbon on 29th December 1537 to take up his post. Later, as can be confirmed by a letter from King João III to Baltazar de Faria, he was chosen for the post of Ambassador in the Council of Trento, which he did not take[128]. He became Viceroy of India at an old age and died there.

His first wife was Dona Filipa Henriques, daughter of Simão de Miranda Henriques of whom he had no offspring, and his second wife was Dona Helena Mascarenhas, daughter of Dom Pedro Mascarenhas, they also had no children. His heir was Dom João Mascarenhas, his nephew, the defender of the second siege of Diu.

4° — Dom Manuel Mascarenhas will be discussed in I, as he was the progenitor of the Counts of Torre, Marquises of Fronteira and Counts of Conculim.

5° — Dom António Mascarenhas fought in Arzila until 1508, he was captured by the Moors and died there leaving no descendants.

6° — Dona Isabel Henriques married Dom João Coutinho, second Count of Redondo.

7° — Dona Leonor Henriques married Simão Freire de Andrade, Lord of Bobadela.

I

Dom Manuel Mascarenhas, fourth son of King João II's Captain of the Ginetes, Comendador of Rosmaninhal, Governor and Captain-General of Arzila, from 1538 to 1545, substituting his brother-in-law, Count of Redondo. In 1515 Dom Manuel and his brother, Dom João, participated in the conquest of Azamor in Dom Jaime, the Duke of Bragança's fleet. There he earned the nick-name of »cutting sword».

Married to Dona Leonor de Sousa Palha (or Pala), daughter and heiress of Francisco Palha (or Pala) of Santarém, Lord of Goucharia and Chantas, and of his second wife Dona Maria de Sousa. He was Alcaide-mor of Fronteira and third Lord of the estates of Goucharia and Chantas, they had the following children:

1° — Dom Fernando Mascarenhas — see II.

2° — Dom Francisco Mascarenhas, Comendador of Cacurrais of the Order of Christ, Counsellor to King Sebastião and King Henrique, General of Malabar and of the Indian Sea, Governor and Captain-General of Ormuz.

He married Dona Jerónima de Castro Lima e Herrera, daughter of Jorge Lima e Herrera, General of the Indian Sea and of the Portuguese Armada, and of Dona Isabel de Castro Lima e Pereira, they had a son and a daughter.

a) Dom Jorge Mascarenhas, first Count of Castelo Novo and first Marquis of Montalvão, Viceroy of Brazil, Governor of Mazagão, Mayor of Lisbon, etc. He had eleven children by his wife, Dona Francisca de Vilhena, one of which was Dom Jerónimo Mascarenhas, Bishop of Segovia and author of *História da Cidade de Ceuta*.

b) Dona Isabel de Castro e Vilhena, who married Dom João Soares de Alarcão e Melo, seventh Alcaide-mor of Torres Vedras, Master of Ceremonies of the Royal House of Portugal, etc. They had several children, one of whom was Count of Torres Vedras and Marquis of Trocifal.

3° — Dom Vasco Mascarenhas died in Arzila fighting the Moors.

4° — Dona Isabel Mascarenhas married Dom Jorge Telo de Menezes, Captain of Sofala, etc.

II

Dom Fernando Mascarenhas, the eldest son of Dom Manuel Mascarenhas, Comendador of Rosmaninhal, fourth Lord of the Goucharia and Chantas estates, Counsellor to King Sebastião, with whom he went to Africa and where both died in the unfortunate battle of Alcácer Quibir on 4th August 1578.

He first married Dona Filipa da Costa, daughter of Gil Eanes da Costa, King João III's Ambassador to the court of Carlos V, Emperor of Germany; Dispatch Minister,etc., and of his second wife, Dona Joana da Silva. They had the following children:

1° — Dom Manuel Mascarenhas — see III.

2° — Dom Vasco Mascarenhas, fought heroically with some of his brothers in India and died on his return voyage to Portugal.

3° — Dom Filipe Mascarenhas died fighting in India.

4° — Dom Francisco Mascarenhas also died fighting in India.

5° — Dona Lourença Mascarenhas married Francisco Carneiro, Captain of the Island of Príncipe and left descendants to the House of the Counts of Lumiares.

6° — Dona Paula Mascarenhas married Dom Duarte da Costa, first cousin of the Count of Soure. They left descendants to this House.

7° — Dom Álvaro da Costa took ecclesiastic vows.

8° — Dona Maria Mascarenhas took monastic vows.

9° — Dona Leonor Mascarenhas took monastic vows.

III

Dom Manuel Mascarenhas eldest son of Dom Fernando Mascarenhas, Counsellor to King Sebastião, Comendador do Rosmaninhal, fifth Lord of the Goucharia and Chantas estates, Governor and Captain-General of Mazagon.

He participated with King Sebastião in the sad battle of Alcácer Quibir where he was wounded and captured. He was one of the few nobles to return to Portugal in exchange for a ransom.

Dom Manuel married Dona Francisca de Ataíde, daughter of Dom Nuno Manoel, second Lord of Atalaia and Tancos, Alcaide-mor of Mourão, and of Dona Joana Ataíde, daughter of Dom

António de Ataíde, first Count of Castanheira and Countess Ana de Távora. They had fifteen children:

1° — Dom Fernando Mascarenhas — see IV.

2° — Dom João Mascarenhas fought in India where he died, a bachelor.

3° — Dom Pedro Mascarenhas entered the Order of São Francisco.

4° — Dom Francisco Mascarenhas fought in India and died there without having married.

5° — Dom Nuno Mascarenhas died when he was still a boy.

6° — Dom Diogo Mascarenhas fought in India, having later on taken monastic vows in the Order of São Francisco.

7° — Dom Filipe Mascarenhas, Governor of Ceylon, Captain-General of India, Viceroy of India from 1645 to 1651 and King's Counsellor.

Dona Maria Coutinho was his wife and the daughter of Dom Diogo Coutinho and Dona Inês Freire of whom he had no children.

He died on his return voyage to Portugal and was buried in Luanda in the Church of the Jesuit School. His niece Dona Helena da Silveira inherited a part of his enormous fortune and with the other part the estate of Conculim was founded for the son of his eldest brother, Dom Fernando, first Count of Torre. This did not come to happen, as you will see.

8° — Dom António Mascarenhas fought in India where he died, a bachelor.

9° — Dona Joana Mascarenhas nun of the Convent of Castanheira.

10° — Dona Filipa Mascarenhas became nun of the Monastary of Castanheira.

11° — Dona Maria Mascarenhas nun of the Convent of Castanheira.

12° — Dona Madalena de Ataíde married Dom António de Almeida, Comendador of Lardosa and Bemposta of the Order of Christ, and left descendents to the House of the Marquises of Lavradio.

13° — Dona Catarina Mascarenhas became nun of the Monastary of Santa Clara in Santarém.

14° — Dona Margarida de Vilhena became nun of the Monastary of Santa Clara in Santarém.

15° — Dona Leonor Mascarenhas became nun of the Monastary of Santa Clara in Santarém.

IV

Dom Fernando Mascarenhas, eldest son of Dom Manuel Mascarenhas, Comendador of the Torre de Fonte Arcada, of Carrazedo and Rosmaninhal of the Order of Christ and sixth Lord of the estates of Goucharia and Chantas.

He was granted the title of first Count of Torre, for eternity («de juro e herdade» with exception to these, one has to ask permission from the King to use any other inherited title), by royal charter on 26th July 1638; Governor and Captain-General of Ceuta and Tangiers where he obtained the well-earned reputation of being a brave soldier; sixteenth Governor and Captain-General of Brazil (1639-1640) [129]; Land and Sea General of the armed forces of Portugal and Castille having been the only Portuguese to belong to both forces during the Castillian domination; member of King João IV's State Council and Council of War; President of the Senate of the Town Hall of Lisbon (1647-1650), etc. He was Commanding Officer of the Armada which went to Brazil to try and recuperate Pernambuco and other fortresses which had fallen into the hands of the Dutch. The fleet was defeated partly by the enemy and partly by a storm which made the Portuguese lose many of their ships. The Count of Torre was held responsible for this great disaster. King Filipe III took away all the titles and honours to which he was entitled and had him encarcerated in the Fort of São Julião da Barra near Lisbon. Meanwhile Portugal won its independence from Spain and Filipe IV having been informed and believing that the «Count of Torre had refuted all King João IV's offers and had induced Fernando de la Cueva to ask for help from the Galicean ports» [130], «burnt the papers concerning the proceedings brought against Dom Fernando, renewed all the favours which had been taken away from him and granted him many more» [131].

Now what had really happened was the opposite: Fernando de la Cueva had handed over the fortress to the Portuguese after the Count of Torre had made him dazzling promises, which helped the mutineers immensely. As a reward for this dedication King João IV gave back all his priviledges and granted him many more.

Dom Fernando died on 9th August, 1651 having been married to Dona Maria de Noronha, daughter of Dom Luís da Silveira, Lord of Sarzedas and Sobreira Formosa and of Dona Joana Lima, their marriage was blessed with the following children:

1° — Dom Manuel Mascarenhas fought bravely in the Battles of Restoration. On 7th February, 1649 Dom Diogo de Eça[132] came home and found him talking to his sister and killed him when he refused to marry her immediately.

2° — Dom João Mascarenhas became second Count of Torre and should have inherited the estate of Conculim from his uncle Dom Filipe, but instead it went to his third son. See V.

3° — Dom Pedro Mascarenhas died a young boy.

4° — Dona Jerónima Mascarenhas, died a young girl.

5° — Dona Francisca Mascarenhas, lady of the court in Madrid, where she died without having married.

6° — Dona Eufrásia Filipa de Noronha married Dom Francisco de Sousa, first Marquis of Minas and third Count of Prado. Their son, the second Marquis of Minas and fourth Count of Prado and grandson of the first Count of Torre was the famous General of the Wars of Succession who conquered Madrid.

7° — Dona Helena de Noronha married Dom Francisco Luís da Gama, second Marquis of Niza and sixth Count of Vidigueira.

8° — Dona Margarida Luísa de Noronha married Dom Pedro de Almeida de Portugal, 32nd Viceroy of India and first Count of Assumar.

V

Dom João Mascarenhas became second Count of Torre for eternity and first Marquis of Fronteira, granted by charter on 7th January, 1670 by Prince Pedro. He was Comendador of Rosmaninhal, Sant'Iago da Fonte Arcada, S. Nicolau de Carrazedo, S. João de Castelão, S. Martinho de Cambres, S. Martinho de Pindo all of them belonging to the Order of Christ, seventh Lord of the estates of Goucharia and Chantas, Lord of the estates of Conculim and Verodá in India, Member of King Pedro II's State Council and Council of War; Mestre de Campo General of the provinces of Estremadura and Minho; Cavalry General in the province of Alentejo and Grand Prior of Crato of the Order of S. João de Malta.

He was one of the great war generals of the Wars of Restoration, mainly in the battles of Ameixial (8th July, 1663) and Montes Claros (17th June, 1665), where he fought valiantly as Mestre de Campo General.

Father Manuel Bernardes[133] referred to his legendary strength in the following way: «No one can deny the force of the arm and sword of the Count of Torre, first Marquis of Fronteira, which in one blow could cut off the head a bull. This was witnessed in the public games played in front of the palace; where the Sword scratched the ground after having killed the beast, an event which was described by a certain wit in the following sonnet:

Foi para o raio de aço curta esphera
A vida de um só bruto limitada;
Queixa-se da materia a cutilada;
Mais fundo entrara, se mais fundo houvera
Torna (se pódes) a viver, ó fera;
Vai busca mais pescoços à manada,
Que no resto das iras desta espada
Nova morte sem nova acção te espera.
Mas, já que ao ferro do melhor Mavorte,
Depois de sorver vidas, inda dura
Vasta e anhelante a sêde de seu córte,

Que empregos achará força tão dura?
Rasgue o boi, e obra a terra; desta sorte
Sae da sobras da morte a sepultura.»

Prince Pedro favoured him and the Count of S.João and «took their advice is if it were indispensable».[134]

A lampoon of the time «which was affixed in most prominent places of the court»[135], said:

Se o Príncipe governar
Should the Prince come to rule
Quiser com satisfação
With much satisfaction he could
Meta o S. João na Torre
Put S.João in the Tower
E o Tôrre em S.Gião.
And Tôrre in S. Gião.

As usual, favouritisms made the opposition reveal itself and try and make them fall into disgrace.

Dom João married Dona Madalena on 19th July, 1651, she was the daughter of Francisco de Sá e Meneses, third Count of Penaguião and his wife Dona Joana de Castro, daughter of the sixth Counts of Atouguia. He died on 16th July 1681. They had the following children:

1° — Dom Fernando Mascarenhas, second Marquis of Fronteira and third Count of Torre. See VI.

2° — Dom Filipe Mascarenhas died in 1665 at the age of seven and therefore did not inherit the County of Conculim.

3° — Dom Francisco Mascarenhas, heir to the estates of Conculim and Verodá in India, founded by Dom Filipe Mascarenhas. As a reward for services rendered by his uncle, Viceroy Dom Filipe, King Pedro II granted him and his descendents the title of Count of Conculim by charter on 3rd June,

1676. He was called the Prince of Latin Poetry on account of his erudition. According to Barbosa Machado «he wrote letters in Latin with the purity of Cicero's sentences and the elegance of Plinium's concepts».

In 1682 he belonged to the famous fleet who left the port of Lisbon to escort the Duke of Savoy, Dona Isabel's future husband and was one of the people who most distinguished themselves on this expedition.

He married his cousin, Dona Maria Josefa de Noronha, daughter of the fourth Count of Vidigueira and second Marquis of Niza. This title belongs today to the present Count of Torre and Marquis of Fronteira, as well as the County which is still in the hands of the representatives of this family, as this branch of the family became extinct in 1755.

Dom Francisco was also Counsellor to King Pedro II, Comendador of S. João de Castelãos and S. Martinho de Cambres, of the Bishopric of Lamego, S. Martinho de Pinho, Viseu, etc.

4° — Dona Isabel de Castro maried her cousin Dom João de Almeida, second Count of Assumar.

5° — Dona Francisca de Castro took monastic vows at the Monastry of Cardiais where she became Prioress.

6° — Dona Joana de Castro died a young girl.

VI

Born on 4th December, 1655, Dom Fernando Mascarenhas, second Marquis of Fronteira, third Count of Torre for eternity, 8th Lord of the estates of Goucharia and Chantas, donee of the Mordomia-Mor (Mordomo-mor = Lord Chamberlain of the King's household) of Faro with certain royal priviledges, Comendador of Santiago de Torres Vedras, of the Patriarchate of Lisbon, S. Nicolau de Carrazedo and S. Miguel de Linhares, of the Archbishopric of Braga, Fonte Arcada, of the Bishopric of Porto, Rosmaninhal and Guarda; patron of the Monastary of S. Domingos da Serra of the Order of Pregadores and of Nossa Senhora da Conceição da Torre das Vargens, where he owned an county.

He became Governor and Captain General of the Kingdom of Algarve, Mestre de Campo General and Governor of the Province of Beira, Arms Governor of the province of Alentejo, Counsellor to King João V, president of the High Court, one of the first censors of the Royal History Academy and also its President where everyone admired «the elegance of his concise and sublime style, such was it that the concision did not degenerate into darkness nor the sublimeness into a precipice»[136].

A learned man, «from the beginning this genius cultivated the Liberal Arts, although it did seem that most his erudition was inherited and not acquired from studying»[137], thus refers Dom António Caetano de Sousa[138] to him. «He was Minister of great integrity and talent, helpful and very knowledgable in ancient and modern history and Latin, his writing was elegant in Latin or in Portuguese as can be seen in the books of the Academy which were printed; here he was entrusted with the History of the Romance, for which he wrote,

with admirable method, a few chapters in Portuguese which he used with eloquence and purity. He was undoubtedly one of the erudite men of his time and a great Minister at his Majesty's service».

He left more than a dozen works of great historical interest, some of them were published in the Collection of the Documents of the Royal Academy.

In the Wars of Succession he entered Castille, with the Marquis of Minas, who was the first general to occupy Madrid. He died on 25th February, 1729, and was burried in the Church of Chagas.

Dona Joana Leonor de Toledo e Meneses, daughter of Dom Jerónimo de Ataíde, seventh Count of Atouguia and Countess Leonor de Meneses was his wife and gave him the following children:

1° — Dom João Mascarenhas, third Marquis of Fronteira and fourth Count of Torre, see VII.

2° — Dom Francisco Xavier Mascarenhas, boarder at the Royal College of S. Paulo of the Coimbra University and Lord Treasurer of the Guarda See. Having exchanged ecclesiastical life for the military one, he left for India on 7th May, 1740, on the Nossa Senhora do Carmo with the rank Sargento-mor de Batalha (First Battle Sargent) at the time of Dom Luís de Meneses, first Marquis of Louriçal, was Viceroy. It was due to him that the proud ruler Bonsulo was defeated, surrendering the Fortresses of Carjuem and Culuale and the province of Barden was also recuperated.

Francisco José Freire published an Historical Eulogy of Dom Francisco's virtuous and military deeds. He died in Goa on 11th September, 1745 and was buried at the foot of the alter of the church of S. Francisco Xavier, as requested in his will.

3° — Dom António Mascarenhas, also a boarder at the Royal College of S. Paulo of the University of Coimbra, Canon of the See of Braga, he also exchanged the ecclesiastical life for the army one and died in Almeirim on 16th April, 1725.

4° — Dom Luís Mascarenhas, a boarder at the same college as his brothers and Abbot of S. Martinho in the Archbishopric of Braga. He too abandoned the ecclesiastical life for the military one where he rose to the rank of Captain-General. He became Governor of the province of S. Paulo, Counsellor to King José, Member of Parliament for the Union of the Three States, Alcaide-Mor of Guimarães and Viceroy of India from 1754 to 1756 when he was granted the title of Count of Alva. Dom Luís was married to Dona Maria Barbara de Meneses, daughter of the second Counts of Santiago and died in India fighting against the King of Sunda, in Pondá on 26th June, 1756.

5° — Dom José Mascarenhas died a young boy.

6° — Dom Jerónimo Mascarenhas died a young boy.

7° — Dona Luísa de Meneses died a young girl.

8° — Dona Teresa de Meneses died a young girl.

9° — Dona Madalena de Meneses took monastic vows in the Order of S. Domingos in the Convent of the Sacramento de Lisboa.

10° — Dona Isabel de Meneses took monastic vows in the Order of S. Domingos in the Convent of the Sacramento de Lisboa.

11° — Dona Maria de Meneses became a nun in the Convent of Santa Clara in Santarém.

12° — Dona Inocência de Meneses took monastic vows in the Monastery of Esperança in Lisbon.

13° — Dona Leonor de Meneses married the second Count of São Tiago, Aleixo de Sousa da Silva e Meneses, they left descendents.

14° — Dona Antónia de Meneses became a nun, as did her sister Dona Inocência, at the Convent of Esperança.

VII

Dom João Mascarenhas, third Marquis of Fronteira, fourth Count of Torre for eternity, Lord of Fronteira, ninth Lord of the Estates of Goucharia and Chantas, Comendador of Rosmaninhal, Santiago de Fonte Arcada, S. Nicolau de Carrazedo, Santa Cristina de Afife, S. Miguel de Linhares and Santiago de Torres Vedras. He was born on 19th February, 1679, in the parish of Encarnação and died on 12th April, 1737.

In the army he reached the rank of Captain-General and served with distinction in America and Africa. He married on 13th August, 1713 Dona Helena de Lencastre, daughter of Dom Luís de Lencastre, fourth Count of Vila Nova de Portimão and his wife the Countess Madalena Teresa de Noronha, daughter of Dom Estevão de Meneses and Dona Helena de Noronha who in turn was the daughter of the third Counts of Arcos. They had the following children:

1° — Dona Madalena de Lencastre married Dom Luís Guedes de Miranda, 14th Lord of Murça and Captain of the Dragoons.

2° — Dom Fernando Mascarenhas, fourth Marquis of Fronteira and fifth Count of Torre — see VIII.

3° — Dona Joana de Lencastre died a young girl.

4° — Dom José Mascarenhas became fifth Marquis of Fronteira and sixth Count of Torre because his brother, Dom Fernando, left no heir — see IX.

5° — Dom Luís Mascarenhas died a young boy.

6° — Dona Maria de Lencastre died a young girl.

7° — Dom Manuel Mascarenhas died a young boy.

8° — Dona Teresa de Lencastre died a young girl.

VIII

Dom Fernando Mascarenhas, fourth Marquis of Fronteira, fifth Count of Torre for eternity, Lord of Fronteira, tenth Lord of the Estates of Goucharia and Chantas, Comendador of Rosmaninhal and with five more offices in the Order of Christ, Captain of the Court's horses, Member of Parliament for the Union of the Three States, Lord of several Alcadarias-Mores and Patronages of this House, Inspector of the House of Queen Mariana Vitória, etc. He was born on 16th August, 1717 and died on 14th August, 1765.

On 7th October, 1737, he married Dona Ana de Lencastre, daughter of Dom Pedro de Lencastre Silveira Valente Castelo Branco Vasconcelos Barreto e Meneses, fifth Count of Vila Nova de Portimão and Countess Maria Sofia de Lencastre, daughter of Rodrigo Anes de Sá, third Marquis of Abrantes and Marchioness Isabel de Lorena, in turn daughter of Dom Nuno Álvares Pereira de Melo, first Duke of Cadaval and his second wife, Duchess Maria Angelina Henriqueta Catarina de Lorena, also daughter of Francisco de Lorena, Count of Harcout de Reims, Prince of Harcanot, Caçador-mor (Master of the Hunt) of France and his wife, Princess Catarina Henriqueta, daughter of Henri, fourth King of France.

The Marchioness died giving birth to their only daughter, Dona Maria Mascarenhas, who also died a few months later.

According to Dom António Caetano de Sousa's *Memórias Históricas e Genealógicas dos Grandes de Portugal* (Historical and Genealogical Memoires of the Important Families of Portugal), the Marquis was to have taken his cousin, Dona Madalena Xavier dos Passos Mascarenhas, for his second wife. She was the daughter and heiress of the third Counts of Conculim as her only brother had died a bachelor on 20th July, 1792 leaving no descendents, however, this marriage never took place.

The House of Conculim, therefore passed into the hands of the Marquises of Fronteira who were the closest relatives, where it remains to date. In the interesting memoires written by Dom José Trazimundo Mascarenhas Barreto, Marquis of Fronteira and Alorna: «My family, as is already known, was my Mother...a number of servants, some of them inherited from the House of the Counts of Conculim, making a total of more than eighty people amongst governesses and servants»[139].

IX

Dom José Luís Mascarenhas, fourth son of the third Marquis of Fronteira, who succeeded his brother who left no descendents, became fifth Marquis of Fronteira, sixth Count of Torre for eternity, sixth Count of Conculim, Lord of Conculim and Verodá in India, Lord of Fronteira, eleventh Lord of the Estates of Goucharia and Chantas, Comendador of Rosmaninhal and another five offices of the Order of Christ, Queen Mariana Victória's Inspector and later of the Princess of Brazil,etc. He was born on 14th March, 1721 and died on 25th March, 1799.

When his brother, Dom Fernando, died leaving no descendents he abandoned the ecclesiastical life where he was Canon of the Holy Patriarchal Church and was granted special authorization to marry and give continuity to such an illustrious family.

On 30th February, 1771, he married Dona Mariana Josefa de Vasconcelos e Sousa, daughter of José Vasconcelos e Sousa, fifth Count of Castelo Melhor and of Calheta and first Marquis of Castelo Melhor and his wife Marchioness Maria Rosa de Noronha, daughter of Dom António de Noronha e Albuquerque, second Marquis of Angeja and his wife Marchioness Luísa Josefa de Meneses, daughter of the fourth Counts of Tarouca. They had two children:

1° — Dom João José Luís Mascarenhas Barreto, sixth Marquis of Fronteira and seventh Count of Torre. —See X.

2° — Dona Maria Teresa Josefa de Vasconcelos Mascarenhas died without having married.

X

Dom João José Luís Mascarenhas Barreto, sixth Marquis of Fronteira, seventh Count of Torre for eternity, seventh Count of Conculim, Lord of Conculim and Verodá in India, Lord of Fronteira and of Torre das Vargens, twelfth Lord of the Estates of Goucharia and Chantas, donee of the Mordomado-Mor of Faro, Princess Maria Benedita's Inspector and Captain of the Cavalry. He was born on 13th January, 1778 and died at the age of twenty eight on 24th February, 1806.

He was Comendador of S. Miguel de Linhares, Santiago de Fonte Arcada, Nossa Senhora do Rosmaninhal, Santa Cristina de Afife, S. Nicolau de Carrazedo all of the Order of Christ. On 10th November, 1799 he married Dona Leonor Benedita de Oyenhausen e Almeida, who was born in the city of Oporto on 30th November, 1776 and died on 18th October, 1850. She was heiress to the titles and assets of the House of Alorna, being the eldest daughter of Dona Leonor de Almeida Portugal de Lorena e Lencastre [140], fourth Marchioness of Alorna and eighth Countess of Assumar, Countess d'Oyenhausen-Gravenbourg in Austria by marriage, and because to her only brother, the Count d'Oyenhausen João Ulrico, died on 14th August, 1822 aged twenty nine years.

They had the following children:

1° — Dom José Trazimundo Mascarenhas Barreto, seventh Marquis of Fronteira and eighth Count of Torre. — See XI.

2° — Dom Carlos Mascarenhas — see XIII.

3° — Dona Leonor Juliana Mascarenhas married, on 6th February, 1826, Dom Vicente de Sousa Coutinho Monteiro Paim, fourth Count of Alva. She was born on 4th April, 1804 and died on 3rd February, 1841. Their only son, Dom Luís José Maria de Sousa Coutinho Monteiro Paim, was born on 19th April, 1827, and died a bachelor leaving no heirs.

XI

Dom José Trazimundo Mascarenhas Barreto, seventh Marquis of Fronteira, eighth Count of Torre for eternity, eighth Count of Conculim and succeeding his maternal grandmother[(141)], fifth Marquis of Alorna and fourth Count of Assumar, Count of Oyenhausen-Gravenbourg of Austria, Lord of Conculim and Verodá in India; Lord of Fronteira and Torre das Vargens, thirteenth Lord of the Estates of Goucharia and Chantas; Peer of the realm, Field Marshal, General Commander of the National Batallions, Mayor of Lisbon, Lord Chamberlain of the Households of the Queens Estefania and Maria Pia; Grã-Cruz of the old and noble Order of the Torre Espada do Valor Lealdade e Mérito; Knight of the same order for the part he played in the Battle of Ponte Ferreira and officer for the Battle of Aceiceira; Grã-Cruz of the Order of Christ for Carlos III in Spain, S. Gregório Magno of Rome, S. Maurício and S. Lázaro of Italy, the Red Eagle of Prussia, of Albert the Brave of Saxon, of the Rose of Brazil, etc. According to a royal letter dated 15th July, 1867, he held the position of Condestável of the Kingdom for the

proclamation of King Fernando as Regent.

As aide-de-camp to the General, Count of Vila Flor, he was one of the heroes of Mindelo and one of the people who most distinguished themselves in the Liberal Campaignes. As a reward for services rendered, King Luís wanted to grant him the title of Duke, but the Marquis excused himself saying «if he had indeed been of service to his country, he had already been well rewarded». He left interesting *Memoires* published in five volumes, revised and organized by Ernesto de Campos de Andrada. He was born on 4th January, 1802 and died in Benfica on 19th February, 1881.

On 14th February, 1821, he married Dona Maria Constança da Câmara, Maid of Honour to Queen Maria II, Queen Estefânia and Queen Maria Pia, sister of the first Count of Taipa, daughter of Dom Luís Gonçalves da Câmara Coutinho, Lord of the Deserted Islands, of the Estates of Taipa and Regalados, Alcaide-Mor of Torres Vedras, and had been granted several awards, etc., and Dona Maria de Noronha, daughter of the seventh Count of Arcos. One daughter was born to them:

1° — Dona Maria Mascarenhas Barreto, eighth Marchioness of Fronteira and ninth Countess of Torre for eternity. — See XII.

XII

Dona Maria Mascarenhas Barreto, eighth Marchioness of Fronteira, sixth Marchioness of Alorna, ninth Countess of Torre for eternity, ninth Countess of Conculim, tenth Countess of Assumar, Countess of

Oyenhausen-Gravenbourg of Austria, Maid of Honour to the Queen Estefânia and Queen Maria Pia, Lady of Conculim and Verodá in India, as well as all of her Father's other assets and awards. She was born on 27th May, 1822 and died on 30th April, 1914.

She married on 12th May, 1856 to Pedro João Morais Sarmento, second Baron of Torre de Moncorvo, son of the first Vicount and first Baron of Torre de Moncorvo, who was permitted to use his wife's titles.

Dom Pedro was Peer of the Realm, Oficial-Mor of the Royal House, King Luís' Chamberlain, Comendador of the Order of Christ, Knight of the Sovereign Order of São João de Jerusalém, Officer the Order of Leopold of Belgium, Second Secretary of the Legation, etc.

The Marquis of Fronteira, accompanied the King of Sion, Pararmindo Mahachulalongkon who adopted the title of Rama V, when he visited Portugal in 1897 on a trip through Europe. As a token of his gratitude the King gave him a salver made of silver coins from his country, and invested him with the Order of the White Elephant. The King left a gift of one thousand Reis for the Marquis to distribute amongst the poor of Lisbon.

No children were born of this marriage and the titles and assets were inherited by Dom Carlos Mascarenhas. — See XIII.

XIII

Dom Carlos Mascarenhas, Peer of the Realm, Chamberlain and Aide-de-Camp to King Pedro V, Commander of the Municipal Guards of Lisbon and later of the Cavalry Regiment of Lancers, Aide-de-Camp of the Duke of Terceira, Oficial de Ordens (Orders Officer) to the Duke of Bragança, Dom Pedro, Grã-Cruz of the Orders of S. Bento de Aviz, of Carlos III of Spain, Albert the Brave of Saxon, Comendador and Officer of the Torre e Espada, honoured thrice on the battlefield, in Spain, defending the throne of Queen Isabel II, in the Battles of Valmosêda, Arlaban, Conchas and Arminon. He was born on 2nd April, 1803 and died on 3rd May, 1861.

On behalf of the Regent and the people of the Azores Islands, in August 1831 he, Teotónio de Ornellas Bruges Avila Paim da Câmara de Noronha Ponce de Leon and Manuel de Sousa Raivoso were part of a delegation who went to England to pay hommage, obedience and loyalty to the Queen and the ex-Emperor of Brazil on their arrival in Europe. At the age of thirty one he was invited to take the post of Viceroy of India, which he refused[142].

He died with the rank of Brigadier having been one of the officers who most distinguished themselves at the time and one of King Pedro IV's important collaborators in the Liberal Campaigns.

He had the following six children:

1° — Dona Eugénia Carlota Mascarenhas married Paulo de Jesus Burguete and of whom we have no more information.

2° — Dom Carlos Mascarenhas died a young boy.

3° — Dona Maria Luísa Mascarenhas died a young girl.

4° — Dom João Maria Mascarenhas died a young boy.

5° — Dom José Maria Mascarenhas, ninth Marquis of Fronteira and tenth Count of Torre. — See XIV.

6° — Dona Leonor Maria de Assis Mascarenhas was born on 24th November, 1853 and married António José de Ávila e Bolama, second Count of Ávila, Peer of the Realm, Division General, Member of Parliament, General Director of the Kingdom's Geodesic and Topographical Works, etc., nephew of the first Duke of Ávila and Bolama, and son of Manuel José de Ávila and Dona Maria Leonor de Almeida e Silva. She inherited from her cousin Dona Maria Mascarenhas Barreto, eighth Marchioness of Fronteira, of the Palace of S. Domingos de Benfica, of the Herdade of Torres Vedras, part of the County of Conculim in India, etc. Dom José Maria Mascarenhas, her brother's eldest son was named her heir as she had no children. She died on 17th February, 1923.

XIV

Dom José Mascarenhas, ninth Marquis of Fronteira, seventh Marquis of Alorna, tenth Count of Torre for eternity, tenth Count of Conculim, eleventh Count of Assumar, Count of Oyenhausen-Gravenbourg in Austria, titles which he never used, he became heir to his first cousin, Dona Maria Mascarenhas Barreto, eighth Marchioness of Fronteira, of Goucharia, Chantas and many other 'herdades' in the Provinces of Santarém and Almeirim and of part of the County of Conculim in India, etc.

He was born on 14th August, 1856 and died in Paço de Arcos, near Lisbon, on 26th January, 1930, having married Dona Carlota Pinto, daughter of João Pinto and Dona Luísa Antónia Pinto. They had the following children:

1° — Dom José Maria Mascarenhas, tenth Marquis of Fronteira and eleventh Count of Torre. — See XV.

2° — Dona Luísa Mascarenhas was born on 19th November, 1883 and died on 7th November, 1936 in Paço de Arcos. She maried José de Lencastre Laboreiro Fiuza, landowner, son of Joaquim Fiuza and Dona Maria Isabel de Vilalobos de Lencastre Laboreiro and they had children.

3° — Dom Carlos Mascarenhas was born on 19th December, 1888 and was a landowner, he married his first cousin Dona Lucília Fernandes, daughter of Manuel Fernandes and Dona Constança Pinto and they also had children.

4° — Dom António Mascarenhas was born on 6th June, 1893 and died a bachelor on 20th April, 1916.

5° — Dom Alexandre Mascarenhas was born on 3rd February, 1894, was a landowner and married Dona Emília Sanchez who died on 23rd August, 1944, of whom he had children.

6° — Dom João Mascarenhas was born on 14th April, 1896, landowner, he married Dona Teresa Pinto, they had no children.

XV

Dom José Maria Mascarenhas, was born on 3rd November, 1882 and was tenth Marquis of Fronteira, eighth Marquis of Alorna, eleventh Count of Torre for eternity, eleventh Count of Conculim, twelfth Count of Assumar, Count of Oyenhausen-Gravenbourg in Austria, he was heir to his aunt, Dona Leonor Maria de Assis Mascarenhas by marriage, second Marchioness of Ávila and Bolama, of the Palace of S. Domingos de Benfica, the estate of Torre das Vargens, Quinta das Chantas, etc.

A firm monarchist and nonconformist, of vigorous disposition and who throughout his life fought to defend his King and his ideals. His bravery was legendary and a few centuries back he would have gone into battle as many of his forefathers had done and would have written a some brilliant pages of our history.

He followed his friend, Commander Henrique Paiva Couceiro (who, in his will, left him his ring with the coat of arms) in all his attempts to reinstate the monarchy in Portugal. For this he was condemned to maximum penalty and exile, having lived in France for four years (1914-1918) with many other Portuguese who were there for the same reasons, a few of them his relatives.

He ordered the publication of the excellent *Memórias do Sétimo Marquês de Fronteira e d'Alorna* (Memoires of the seventh Marquis of Fronteira and Alorna) at the Imprensa da Universidade de Coimbra, which were revised and organized by Ernesto de Campos de Andrada. These were crucial for study of most of the nineteenth century. On 25th June, 1908 he married Dona Julieta da Serra Penalva, daughter of Ezequiel Augusto de Sousa Penalva, landowner and Dona Júlia Garcia Moreira da Serra. He died on 9th April, 1944, with four children:

1° — Dona Leonor Maria Penalva Mascarenhas was born in the parish of Benfica on 11th April, 1907. She married in the same parish in the chapel of the Palácio Fronteira on 7th January, 1933, José Cassiano Neves, a doctor in medecine, graduated from the University of Lisbon and author of this book, having had children.

2° — Dom Fernando Mascarenhas, eleventh Marquis of Fronteira, and twelfth Count of Torre. —See XVI.

3° — Dona Maria Luísa Penalva Mascarenhas was born in S. Jean de Luz, France, on 25th November, 1917. She married José Manuel do Amaral Pyrrait, landowner and poet, on 15th February, 1938 in the chapel of the Palácio Fronteira. They had children.

4° — Dom António Mascarenhas. —See XVIII.

XVI

Dom Fernando Mascarenhas, eleventh Marquis of Fronteira, ninth Marquis of Alorna, twelfth Count of Torre, twelfth Count of Conculim, thirteenth Count of Assumar, Count of Oyenhausen-Gravenburg in Austria, Lord of the Palácio of S. Domingos of Benfica, of the Estate of Torre das Vargens, etc. He was born in the parish of Benfica on 18th October, 1910.[He belonged to the Grupo de Forcados de Santarém and was a brilliant car driver.] He died in a car accident on August 5, 1956 in Madrid. On 7th July, 1938 he married Dona Maria Margarida de Sousa Canavarro de Menes Fernandes Costa in the chapel of the Palácio Fronteira, they had an only son:

1° — Dom Fernando José Mascarenhas, 13th Count of Torre. — See XVII.

XVII

Dom Fernando José Mascarenhas, twelfth Marquis of Fronteira, tenth Marquis of Alorna, thirteenth Count of Torre for eternity, thirteenth Count of Conculim, fourteenth Count of Assumar, [representative of the titles of the Count of São João da Pesqueira, Count of Alvor and Marquis of Távora, and Portuguese representative of the title of Count of Oyenhausen-Gravenburg in Austria, Lord of the Palácio de S. Domingos de Benfica, of the Estate of Torre das Vargens, etc. He was born in the parish of S. Sebastião da Pedreira, in Lisbon on 17th April, 1945 and took a degree in Philosophy at the Arts Faculty of the University of Lisbon. In 1963 and 1969 he participated in the Students Movements, he belonged to the Movimento Democrático Português (Portuguese Democratic Movement) in the elections of 1969 and afterwards in the Movimento de Oposição Democrática (Democratic Movement of Opposition). After the Revolution of 25th April 1974, he became a member and the Interim General Secretary of the Movimento Social Democrático (Social Democratic Movement). From 1979 to 1988 he tought at the University of Évora. Dom Fernando is the founder and the President of the Board of Trustees of the Fundação das Casas de Fronteira e Alorna. On 13th August, 1969 he married his first wife, Dona Isabel Cardigos dos Reis and his second marriage to, Dona Mafalda Osório Teixeira Rebelo Miquelino took place on 13th August, 1984. She took a B.A. in Sculpture and M.A. in Painting at the Escola de Belas Artes de Lisboa. They have no descendents.]

XVIII

Dom António Mascarenhas was born in the parish of Benfica on 6th August, 1918 and died on 29th January, 1981. He married Dona Madalena Sotto Mayor Pinto Basto in the chapel of the Casa de Fronteira (in Belas near Lisbon) on 13th May, 1944 and they had the following children:

1° — Dom José Maria Pinto Basto Mascarenhas. — See XIX.

2° — Dona Maria Madalena Pinto Basto Mascarenhas married Collin Hogg, Professor at the University of Oxford, they had children.

3° — Dona Leonor Maria Pinto Basto Mascarenhas married Francisco da Fonseca Felner da Costa and they have children.

4° — Dom João Maria Pinto Basto Mascarenhas married Cristina Ribeiro Rocha Homem and they have children.

XIX

Dom José Maria Pinto Basto Mascarenhas was born on 10th March, 1945 and married Maria da Assunção de Castro Infante da Câmara, they had the following children:

1° — Marta Maria Infante da Câmara Mascarenhas.

2° — Maria Infante da Câmara Mascarenhas.

3° — António Maria Infante da Câmara Mascarenhas.

Rococo Stuccoes and Tiles in the Palace of Fronteira

JOSÉ MECO

Built in the second half of the seventeenth century on the site of an earlier construction, the Palace possesses basic decorative elements that date mainly to that period – most especially its tile work. The palace was originally conceived as a country house, and became the main residence of the family of the Marquises of Fronteira after the destruction of their Palace in Lisbon due to the earthquake in 1755. With the Marquis's arrivalthe house was enlarged and its ornamentation elaborated, giving it a new style.

The Palace's decoration, which includes an important body of ornamentation in Pombaline, a Portuguese style of the second half of the eighteenth century, and also a number of rococo works, is all of great importance. This decorative work often goes unnoticed, however, given the dominant seventeenth-century style of the building.

Italian in style, the Palace of Fronteira is very classical, with an almost square plan. Towers stand at the corners with open loggias between them. These last were enclosed with windows as more interior space was needed and were turned into reception rooms. A major change in the layout of the Palace took place when a lateral wing was constructed after the Lisbon earthquake, around 1765. The addition made it necessary to remodel the patio. Further changes to the Palace included those done on the towers and garden walls, which also date to the Pombeline style of the second half of the eighteenth century.

Major rococo elements in the ornamentation of the Palace include tile and stucco work. While much of this work was done in the seventeenth century, rococo style was also incorporated in construction that took place a hundred or so years later. The tile work in the older parts of the Palace dates to the seventeenth century, but some of the stucco work was changed when the building was remodelled in the late eighteen-hundreds. The resulting blend of architectural styles provides a decorative mix of great interest, most especially in the case of the stucco work. Painting and stucco ornamentation portray maritime scenes, moody and picturesque ruins, and other subjects which anticipated the preoccupations of the Romantic period.

A number of Lisbon's palaces and churches were rebuilt after the earthquake with a blend of earlier and more recent rococo ornamentation, and the Palace of Fronteira is certainly one of the most interesting examples of this practice. We begin with the stucco work at the entrance to the Palace. Although the stucco work along the lateral walls was restored at a later time, the center stucco panels retain much of their rococo characteristics. While there are many elements from different periods, it is the interior of the Palace that is of special interest.

The tile panels on the stair date to the close of the seventeenth century – a fact which is known because the blue used in these tiles does not contain the manganese present in later tile work. Although this work was done late in the seventeenth century, its patterns are almost Baroque in style, which creates a most interesting impression. Even the stairs at the entrance have tiles and balustrades that date to the close of the seventeenth century, while the part above, done in the last half of the eighteenth, is already rococo in style.

The walls in the upper part of the entrance stair are also curious: the stucco has been made to imitate marble – a feature typical of stucco work of the time. It was worked first with glue and then with a spatula to give the stucco a patina and a lasting rigidity. Another example of this can be found at the Sala de Concordia at the Pombal Palace at Oeiras, on the outskirts of Lisbon.

Here at Fronteira Palace there is a graceful addition to the stucco work above the entrance stair: a window, framed in stone and set ajar, gives a perspective of the interior of the Palace. This is an extremely unusual example of *trompe l'oeil*. The part above this, however, features more traditional, though certainly not richer, stucco work. Dominating the central spaces, this resembles the traditional pattern of the Portuguese Pombaline pattern of the second half of the eighteenth century. In the framing and in the corners we have a more free and elegant rococo which combines with the framing of the painting in the central portion of the ceiling. The enhancement brought about in its interior spaces through the fine combination of painting and stucco is one of the truly major features of Fronteira Palace.

Stucco had been used at the Convent of Christ in the Portuguese town of Tomar as well as other seventeenth-century churches, and was employed as well at the Convent of Sao Domingos de Benefica, next to Fronteira, to decorate the vault and choir in Mannerist style. Yet this medium only really came to prominence in Portugal with the arrival of rococo. Until the earthquake of 1755, the primary sites where stucco was used for ornament were those in Portuguese India, where it played as important an ornamental role in the surfacing of an interior as tiles played in the surfacing of Portuguese interiors. In Portuguese India stucco was used extensively in churches for interior and exterior ornamentation, and most especially to decorate the vaultings.

Stucco's prominence in Portuguese India was to some extent at least a result of the difficulty of obtaining tiles, which had to be transported there by ship. In continental Portugal, however, stucco only came to be used in conjunction with rococo. It best served the spirit of rococo style where fluid and sinuous lines were required and where execution in stucco was particularly easy. Later, in the neo-classical period, ornamentation became more linear, with less emphasis on volume. Stucco and gold were used less. Tiles, however, adapted well to neo-classical ornamentation.

The Palace of Fronteira was constructed at the time of Portugal's independence from Spain (Portugal had been under spanish domination for the last sixty years). The Count of Torre was made the first Marquis of Fronteira as a reward for his victories in these wars. One of the major rooms at the Palace is the Sala das Batalhas. Along the lower portion of the walls of this room, tile panels commemorating the wars of Restoration were manufactured about 1668.

The upper portion of the Sala das Batalhas, however, was remodelled in the eighteenth century in rococo style and was restored once again in 1915. Unfortunately, much of this recent work was poorly done. While the stucco work is the most monumental feature of the Palace, its poor execution – perhaps largely the result of the 1915 restoration – detracts from its appeal. Stucco is difficult to restore or to maintain in its original beauty, so this failing is to some extent understandable.

The busts in stucco on the walls of the Sala das Batalhas, which represent various members of the Mascarenhas family, are of exceptional interest. These imitate in part the marble-style stucco of other parts of the Palace and are framed by false pilasters. The most interesting part of the Sala das Batalhas is, however, the ceiling, where an array of military equipment is combined with more austere elements. The central portion of the ceiling with its floral display reminds one, in its rigor and repetition, of the characteristically Portuguese rococo Pombaline pattern of tiles. The ceiling is enhanced with curving lines, a shell motif in the corner, and a great diversity of forms, such as, for example, figures playing trumpets.

The central medallion in the ceiling gives the impression of being open to the sky. On a railing around this unusual feature, figures are portrayed flying amidst clouds – a decorative device typical of the period.

Painted stucco work often looses its delicacy when it is repainted. Fortunately, the stucco work in the Sala dos Painéis at Fronteira has never been restored, and thus has a delicacy far superior to that of the Sala das Batalhas. The tile panels in the Sala das Panéis are considered to be the first such panels ordered from Holland. To judge from the themes portrayed in them, it is obvious that the Dutch made these tile panels to order for their clients. While the Dutch did not use tile panels in their own arhchitecture, they must have realised the importance of the Portuguese market, where tile panels were important architectural elements since at least the beginning of the eighteenth century.

Tile panels were made by professionals whose work was technically excellent, though in many instances they omitted elements from the images they were hired to reproduce. The engravings were faithfully copied onto tile, this did not enhance the imagination of the artists and gave the tiles a certain coldness of composition.

These panels play an important role in the history of the Dutch tile panel in Portugal. When tiles were first manufactured in Portugal they were characteristically more primitive and ingenuous, as can be seen in some of the tile panels of the Palace of Fronteira. By the end of the seventeenth century, however, the quality of their images improved, thanks to the efforts of Gabriel del Barco as well as Portuguese masters.

An example of this is furnished by the tiles at the Convento de Sao

Domingos de Benfica. Along with its exemplary seventeenth century mannerist architecture, it has tiles of the same period which are the work of António de Oliveira Bernardes. These are extraordinary for their quality, and are examples of Portuguese tile work at its finest.

The Sala dos Painéis has stucco work in rococo style dating from the second half of the eighteenth century. More delicate than those found in the Sala das Batalhas, they have never been restored and have a delicacy of detail combined with painting. Set in a stucco frame, just as are the rest of the panels in the room, is one painted panel of particular interest. Believed to portray a mill in northeast Brazil, it has nothing to do with any of the other painted panels in the room.

The stucco work that frames each of the doors to the Sala dos Panéis is extremely fine and provides a further setting for the painted panels above them. The ceiling of the room is also finely decorated. The corners and the intervening walls display all the characteristic delicacy of rococo style, though often as not this goes unobserved by a visitor.

It is necessary to give careful observation to these ornaments in order to understand the subtlety of taste at work here, most especially in the case of those ornaments within the central part of the Sala dos Panéis. Especially worthy of mention in this context are the asymmetrically designed stucco frames that surround the painted panels. Flowering branches and other ornamental elements give great elegance to these rooms of the Palace of Fronteira and lend them great delicacy. Here the difference between the decoration of the seventeenth and the eighteenth centuries is on vivid display.

The Sala Império, also called Sala de Juno, does not have tile panels; it does, however, have a ceiling of great interest, which along with the panels above the doors allows the room to maintain the stucco and painting themes to be found in other rooms of the Palace. These panels, though, portray scenes of ruins in what could be called a pre-romantic style. The eighteenth century french painter Jean Baptiste Pillement, who worked in Portugal during three separate visits to the country, is considered to have been responsible for introducing these pre-romantic themes into Portuguese decoration, and might indeed have been the author of these panels.

Another Lisbon palace of the same period as Fronteira is the National Palace of Queluz, where there is a considerable number of paintings of ruins that have also been done in a pre-romantic style. Unlike those of Fronteira, however, many of the panels include exotic figures. These probably derive from Central European sources rather than from the Orient, as has sometimes been suggested. An appreciation of such exotic figures was common to both areas.

Pillement's pre-romantic images, of which the Palace of the Marquis of Fronteira reflects such a marked appreciation, were painted in a number of Portuguese buildings. Although there is no evidence to show that Pillement worked at Fronteira Palace, he did leave disciples who learned his style and who may well have worked there.

The stucco work in the Sala de Juno is different from the stucco work in other rooms of the Palace, where architectural elements tend to be overpowered by the delicacy of the ornamentation. The flowers and vases which decorate the room's walls at midpoint display a very free decorative style. This ornamentation, which includes a series of shell motifs, was an important design element of the period. Typically rococo, these shells are similar to those created in England during this period, where they appeared as gold-carved design elements. While there is great variety in the ornamentation of this period, the themes employed all have common characteristics.

Also integrated into the remodeling of the Palace was the Sala Cor-de-Rosa, also called Sala Intima. It features the first rococo tiles that relate directly to the Palace's stucco work. These tiles depict concerts, afternoon lunches, serenades, and other such gay and elegant activities. These had little to do with the tastes of the period, but the tiles and stucco present them with great charm nevertheless.

Occasionally, there is a link between the themes of the tiles and those of the stucco work, such as that of the ensemble at the Pombal Palace in Oeiras. Here the tiles are in cobalt blue, while in others they are a violet manganese. This is characteristic of Portuguese tile panels: their central portions are painted in one color while their borders are of a variety of others that enrich the one used in the center.

Tiles of the post-earthquake period are characterized by a certain decorative modesty. The original rococo elements possessed exuberance and great originality, while the work done after the earthquake displays more moderation. Moderation also had to be applied to the sumptuous spending that had characterized the reign of Dom Joao V and Dom Jose. The reconstruction of Lisbon after the earthquake was a source of great inspiration, but there was no money to create new buildings. The king's minister, the Marquis of Pombal, had to organize the reconstruction of the city in parts, according to an urban plan. This was one of the first examples of truly organized urban planning in the history of Europe.

This second period was marked by the increasing use of shell-shaped motifs, also known as *concheados*. Whereas the first phase had been characterized by a sense of improvisation, the earthquake gave birth to a kind of planning dictatorship: one which became characteristic of the Pombaline period in general. Stereotyped motifs were copied from engravings, but what made the images in the tile panels interesting was the artist's own interpretation.

Portuguese artists were adept at altering their decorative work, expanding or concentrating elements as the situation demanded. Their work was often rough in conception, and ingenuous in the way in which it was painted, but they were true craftsmen nonetheless, and often taught foreign tile painters.

In the Sala Intima is a magnificent ceiling where the shell motif sets off the ceiling's decoration. If all the empty spaces of the ceiling had been decorated, the effect would have been visually unsatisfying. Instead, the decoration possesses an admirable equilibrium and restraint. Lattice work establishes a repetitive geometric pattern that serves to accentuate the freedom of the other decorative elements.

These characteristics continue in the Smoking Room, where the stucco work gives the central areas a more neo-classical style. Later decoration is adapted to the lower ceilings of these rooms in a similar fashion. The pattern is different, being shaped by two contrasting motifs. Lattice work creates a floral motif at the center of the walls. The floral motifs have a shadow at the base which gives the composition a certain dynamism – a fact that demonstrates the great attention the artist paid to detail.

One ensemble of stucco work, which I would define as pre-Romantic, has ruins, landscapes, and figures, and gives a foretaste of nineteenth century style. Built in the late eighteen-hundreds, this magnificently proportioned room was used alternately as a dining room and bedroom.

Tiles that belong to a late phase of rococo (1785-90) begin to display a different decorative language: here, tile and stucco are more integrated, and relate esthetically to the painting incorporated in it. These tiles are supposed to be the work of Francisco Jorge da Costa, an artist who did much tile work in Brazil, and who bridged the gap between rococo and neo-classical style.

Pedro Alexandrino is another renowned tile artist whose work is featured here. He was the great painter of Lisbon's churches after the earthquake, and he incorporated a significant amount of late Baroque design in his work. Today, however, Alexandrino is not studied much, and so it is necessary to go beyond his well-documented tile work and mention other, lesser known works which, because of their distinctive style and character, can only be assumed to belong to him.

The chapel terrace was constructed in the seventeenth century and has undergone little restoration. On the terrace are tiles that date to an earlier polychrome period, which are set alongside blue and white tiles of a later period. The Palace is a pioneer site for blue tiles: the technical characteristics of these are the same, with blue surrounded by manganese based colors around the center. Only a few of these, however, are in multiple colors, while the rest are primarily in blue or white which in the eighteenth century was braught back in fashion.

The benches on the terrace bear engaging scenes: some are shocking in their candor, while others suggest Hindu motifs which also appear on the base of the chapel's altar. It is very interesting to note how these tiles have been used to fill up empty spaces. Some of the benches are positioned below decorative bands that, with their cartoonish animal and human characters, are reminiscent of twentieth century cartoon art.

The role played by the tile work at the Palace is one of particular fascination. The Palace's architecture, with its Palladian bays and complete arches set against rectangular arches with square ones above, is an exceptional example of Italianate style. Yet the whole of this classical architecture has been turned upside down by the Palace's decorative tiles. A very classical element persists, however, in the materials that were used in its construction. This is an example of Palladian architecture which displays the truly innovative nature of the architecture of the Palace of Fronteira.

Mural paintings at the Palace of Fronteira

MAFALDA OSÓRIO

The Palace of Fronteira has many italianate characteristics, not the least of which is its basic architectural form. At the moment the Palace has no exterior murals, as it did in the past. In the nineteenth century it boasted trompe l'oeil in lozenges, which were very fashionable at the time. This façade was originally built in the eighteenth century, and after being altered was eventually repainted in its original colors. At the time that the trompe l'oeil work was done, all of the arcade along the façade was open as the story above. It is on this second story that one finds Fronteira's finest examples of decorative fresco mural painting.

Looking at the arcade from the outside, the duality of the exterior and interior spaces becomes apparent. In the seventeenth century the palace was probably limited to two towers. The upper story did not yet exist, the lower had no entrance leading to the garden. This structure has a painting which is believed to date to the time the building was enlarged in the eighteenth century.

The first Marquis of Fronteira, who built this house, had very specific tastes, and enjoyed mixing decorative objects gathered from all over the word. This penchant is reflected at Fronteira by the famous Dutch tile panels in the Sala dos Painéis; the Carrara marble which blends in as an architectural accessory; the balustrades, and other secondary elements such as the sculptures of Portuguese marble.

Starting from the entrance to the Palace, a number of eighteenth-century paintings line the walls. The stucco of the ceiling and the painting of the coats of arms were probably done in this century. The marble used in the decoration of the entrance hall is Portuguese as well as from Carrara, and the spheres along the balustrade of the staircase are carved of Alentejo pink marble as is the key stone in diamond shape that stands between the two sets of stairs which lead to the upper hall.

The oval marble fountain at the entrance is within an oval marble framed deep vault surfaced with blue and white tiles in camellia pattern dating from the Palace's construction in the seventeenth century. These same tiles surface the walls along the staircase. Marble enjoyed a great vogue in eighteenth-century Portugal, and the fifth Marquis had the Palace's entire entrance painted to imitate marble to give it a heightened richness of texture. Stucco work was also coming into fashion as a decorative feature for ceilings and frescoes.

In all of the ceilings featuring stucco the figures represented tend to be mythological and symbolic in nature. The gods and heroes of antiquity are shown involved in various familiar – if somewhat haphazardly chosen – pursuits. Why, for example, is Heracles placed in the entrance hall rather than Zeus or another divinity who would relate more directly to the nature of the Palace? Perhaps the reason for Heracles's presence here has something to do with the first Marquis of Fronteira's reputation for strength. He is said, for example, to have decapitated an ox with a sword – an action which has a slightly Heraclean flavor to it. Heracles can be seen on the walls of Fronteira strangling the Nemean lion as the first of his ten labors.

Real and imitation marble are often interestingly juxtaposed at Fronteira, with the rich tones of the real marble – be it Portuguese or Italian – being combined in the painted surfaces. Such is the case, for example, with the *trompe l'oeil* which surrounds a window with a balustrade. Both the stucco and the paint have the same quality of color: soft, pale pastels that are typical of the Baroque in northern Europe. The colors, however, are not always so understated, for instance when gold leaf is applied, darker colors are strategically placed to set off the corners.

In the Sala das Batalhas Dom José Mascarenhas, the fifth Marquis of Fronteira, combined the earlier monochromatic tile panels of the seventeenth century in such a manner that their truly unique nature is highlighted; yet he managed to do this without allowing them to overshadow the splendor of the decorated walls above them.

To catch the eye of those passing below, the eighteenth century stucco of the library ceiling was originally designed as an open loggia. The theme of the stucco here is Hermes, a god associated with science, medicine, and learning: pursuits entirely in keeping with its location. The open gallery next to the gallery is unusual, among other things, for its aviaries, two enormous wall painting representing a cage for birds that is very much in the style of the eighteenth century. The Zoological Garden also includes an aviary which is painted in what some historians have referred to as an infantile perspective.

The open ceiling in the loggia, which one can suppose to date from the eighteenth century, shows birds as they might appear in a book of natural history. One's eye now travels back to the ceiling of the library, which was painted using the tempera technique – a kind of combination of painting and molded stucco. There are also painted bucolic scenes of later date. Various fantastic elements in this work are drawn from a neo-classical Helenism which conforms to stereotypical neo-classical style.

In fresco the artist's paint penetrates the porous surface of a wall rather like a tattoo penetrates human skin, creating an image that can hold up admirably over long periods of time. In addition to its longevity, fresco is remarkable for the unique look which images painted using this technique possess. It is, one might say, a kind of happier version of painting. This particular comparison is by Mestre Lagoa Henriques.

The Sala de Juno is very mysterious, as one half of it dates from the seventeenth century and the other from the eighteenth. Due to damage, a crack was created which very clearly separates the earlier and the later work. On the ceiling Hera, wife of Zeus, sits with a conspicuous crown and in the company of a peacock – a bird characteristically associated with her. Nearby, another human figure, painted at the same time or later, is also visible. Here at Fronteira as elsewhere, the great master-works of eighteenth century Portuguese painting show the influence of the Greek myths.

The stucco decorations in relief in the Sala dos Painéis stand for the different arts: One of these, holding a shepherd's flute and a musical score, is music, while another nearby represents sculpture. In front of these the disciplines of astronomy and geometry are suggested by a collection of instruments. Another stucco features a book and a pen, while the theater is represented by a performer's mask. This room housing all of these works was used for musical performances.

Some of the other paintings in this same room can be roughly dated by the subjects they depict. These include famous battles, ships flying the flag of the National Portuguese Restoration, Dutch ships, and false ruins. The romantic ruins of ancient structures were very popular subjects for painters in late eighteenth century Italy, and the vogue for placing actual ruins in paintings eventually gave birth, in the nineteenth century, to the practice of creating imitation ones. These artificial ruins were in turn made the subject of paintings, such as those included here.

A common decorative element in all of the oil paintings in this room is water. Oil paint applied to a prepared wall and then varnished results in a hardy, long-lasting image. Such works, however, tend to lose their original color as time goes by.

The Drawing Room next to the Sala de Juno, built in the eighteenth century, features painted panels using the same techniques and treating similar motifs as those in the former room: Ocean and river scenes, ships, rock-and-tree-filled landscapes, and moody and mysterious buildings dominate. The stucco work here is less brilliant, but its Baroque ceiling is appealingly exuberant.

A series of private rooms next to the Drawing Room now function for sleeping and dressing. During the time of the fifth Marquis of Fronteira it was customary to have alcoves and small rooms leading to a much more richly decorated area. The smaller rooms had no stucco decoration but oil painting previously protected by varnish. These paintings, very much in the spirit of the period that produced them, depict wild and pastoral scenes populated by hunters, fishermen, and other rustic characters – all of them purely imaginary.

Like others on display elsewhere in the Palace, these fanciful works are rich with water imagery and the mysterious shapes of stone ruins. Tree branches reach skyward, silhouetted against clouds, fiery sunsets, and the distant shapes of mountains. The exuberance of these works surpasses all of the others in the Palace, with the possible exception of those in the Sala das Batalhas.

In terms of color and theme, there is great unity to the paintings in these rooms, the last room, with paintings by Pedro Alexandrino, contains a painting atypical of those at the Palace, though it is a favorite among many painters. It depicts Ares, the god of war, stripped of the military attire made for him by his brother Hephaestus, the Olympian craftsman-god of fire and metalworking. Hephaestus appears here as a very unhappy god indeed. Limping and weak from having been thrown from Olympus by his father Zeus, he does not have the strength to create thunderbolts. Hephaestus was born so ugly that he was sent to the bottom of the sea, where he was taught his trade and sent back to Mount Olympus. Here he built a very large golden throne for his mother, who once seated on it could not get up again. As she was the queen of all the gods and goddesses, a solution was devised by her: give her daughter Aphrodite in marriage to Hephaestus. With Hephaestus married to the beautiful Aphrodite and his wife freed from the golden throne, Zeus became furious, and threw Hephaestus around the world twice. He landed on Mount Etna, where he became established as the god of volcanoes.

In another painting we see sky and clouds: attributes of the goddess Aphrodite, who is shown seated in a carriage drawn by doves. Eros, Aphrodite's son, is shown as well. The name Aphrodite means foamborn: a reference to Aphrodite's birth from the waves of the sea. This appealingly tranquil painting has many fascinating details to analyze.

Another painting shows the judgment of Paris in which, during a banquet, Paris is to give an apple to the most beautiful of the three graces: Athena, first wife of Zeus, Aphrodite, and Hera. Paris, apart from being the son of a king, was particularly handsome, and dedicated to pastoral life. Each of the three goddesses offered him a different reward. Athena offered him success in war, Hera offered him wisdom and success in political life, while Aphrodite, who won the competition, had proposed to provide him with the world's most beautiful woman.

Other scenes include Aeneas escaping with his father following the Trojan war, and Artemis at the pool where Actaeon spied her bathing, in return for which he was turned into a stag and devoured by his hounds. Also included is an image of Pan, the goat-footed son of Hermes, who together with Artemis shared dominion of the world's wild areas. The final scene shows the theft by Hermes, the mischievous god of thieves, of Apollo's cows. Hermes was ultimately forgiven by Apollo for this most famous of his pranks when he bestowed his lyre upon the angry god.

Hermes, in turn, received a gift from Apollo: his magic wand. According to legend this wand was made of gold, and along with the wings given to him by Zeus, which he wore upon his ankles, it is one of this god's main identifying characteristics.

One day Hermes, while pretending to be a shepherd tending his sheep, saw two snakes fighting. Hermes approached them, and the snakes stopped their fighting and wound themselves about his magic wand. Since then this wand has been known for its ability to appease intrigues and anger, and Hermes became the messenger between the world of the living and the world of the dead.

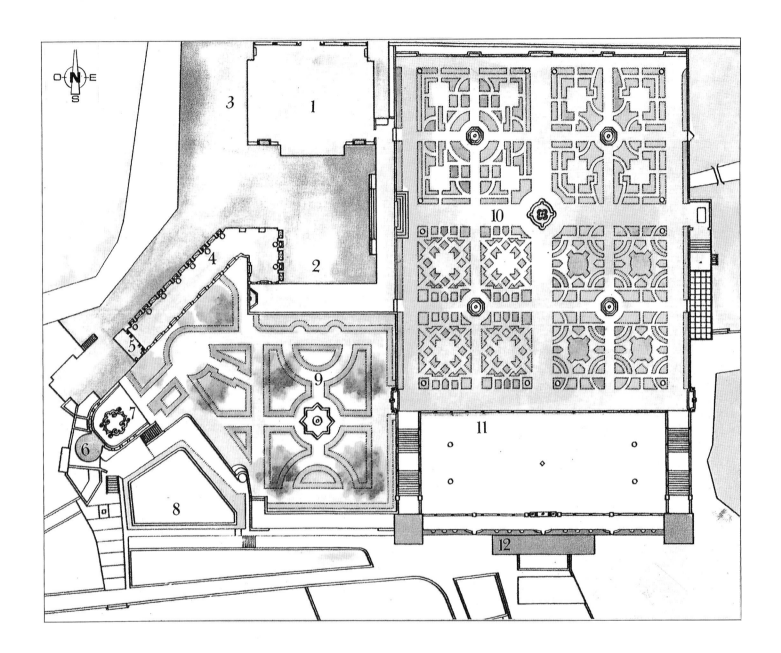

PLAN OF THE GARDEN (Helder Carita)

1. Patio
2. Palace
3. XVIII century wing
4. Terrace in front of the Chapel

5. Chapel
6. Casa do Fresco
7. S tank
8. Pretos lake

9. Garden of Venus
10. Jardim Grande - Classic Garden
11. Large tank
12. Galeria dos Reis

NOTES

(1) Ângelo Pereira, *As Senhoras Infantas*, p. 123.
(2) «Guia de Portugal», *Lisboa e Arredores*, Biblioteca Nacional, p. 427.
(3) «Guia de Portugal», *Op. cit.*, p. 428.
(4) «Guia de Portugal», *Op. cit.*, p. 428.
(5) Ângelo Pereira, *Op. cit.*, p. 123.
(6) «Guia de Portugal», *Op. cit.*, p. 427.
(7) Frei Luís de Sousa, *História de S. Domingos*, vol. III, p. 105, 3rd edition.
(8) Padre António Carvalho da Costa, *Corografia Portuguesa*, 1712, t. III, p. 644.
(9) «Guia de Portugal», *Op. cit.*, p. 423 .
[10] J. M. dos Santos Simões, *Azulejaria em Portugal nos Séculos xv e xvi*, 1990, 2nd edition, p. 216.
(11) H. Scherer, *Histoire du commerce de toutes les nations*, quoted by Francisco Correia, *História Económica de Portugal*, vol. II, p. 6.
(12) Júlio de Castilho, *Lisboa Antiga, O Bairro Alto*, vol. II, pp. 115 and 116, 2nd edition.
(13) Dr. M. Gonçalves Cerejeira, *Clenardo e a Sociedade Portuguesa do seu Tempo*, p. 166.
(14) Le Comte A. Raczynski, *Les arts en Portugal*, Paris, 1846, p. 330.
(15) Le Comte A. Raczynski, *Op. cit.*, p. 427.
(16) José Queirós, *Cerâmica Portuguesa*, p. 234.
(17) Joaquim Rasteiro, *Quinta e Palácio da Bacalhoa em Azeitão*, p. 47.
(18) José Queirós, *Op. cit.*, p. 234.
[19] J. M. dos Santos Simões, *Azulejaria em Portugal no Século xvii*, 1990, t. II, 2nd edition, p. 106.
(20) Joaquim Rasteiro, *Op. cit.*, p. 43.
(21) Joaquim Rasteiro, *Op. cit.*, p. 11.
(22) Gabriel Pereira, *Pelos Subúrbios e Vizinhanças de Lisboa*, p. 210.
(23) Raul Lino, *A Casa Portuguesa*, Exposição de Sevilha.
(24) Esteves Pereira and Guilherme Rodrigues, *Portugal* (historical dictionary), vol. II, p. 286.
(25) Palácio Fronteira archives, now in the Arquivos Nacionais da Torre do Tombo.
(26) *Viaje de Cosme de Médicis por España y Portugal* (1668-1669), edition and notes by Sanchez Rivero, p. 278.

(27) This description of the Quinta de Benfica has already been transcribed by Jorge de Moser in the bulletin of the Museu Nacional de Arte Antiga, 1949, p. 177 and following, which were reprinted in his interesting study «Acerca de uma Tapeçaria».
(28) Alexis Collotes de Jantillet, *Horae Subsecivoe*. Ulyssipone, 1679 (Biblioteca Nacional, Reservados 26). Born in the Duchy of Lorene, he became secretary to Prince Duarte and his friend when he went to Germany, before being taken prisoner and handed over to the Spaniards. Besides *Horae Subsecivoe*, he wrote *Abucilla* which was printed in Ruen, *Helvia Obsidione Liberata*, in Latin, the latter singing the Battle of the Lines of Elvas in prose. In 1662 he was already back in Portugal and was awarded the habit of Christ and an annuity of sixty thousand reis for services rendered to the Prince, as well as the job of «languages officer in the Secretary of State» (Ramos Coelho, *História do Infante D. Duarte*, t. II, p. 727 and t. III, p. 26). I found the original *Horae Subsecivoe* in the Library of Benfica, bound in parchment with the following note in different handwriting: «elegant description of the Quinta of Benfica», as well as several letters in Latin from Alexis Collotes de Jantillet to the second Marquis of Fronteira.
I recently acquired a copy of this rare work, bound in fine skin which was very well preserved.
(29) This refers to the tiling in the Sala dos Painéis. Santos Simões, an expert on the subject tells me in a letter dated 9th September, 1948: «I confirm now that the tile panels in the Sala dos Painéis are in fact of Dutch origin, most likely from the Van Kloets' workshop in Amsterdam, and not only the panel with the boat which was the only one to have attracted my attention. This collection is therefore one of the most remarkable and I would very much like to study them with more time to be able to include them in my book about *Dutch Tiling in Portugal*. As they are mentioned in Jantillet's description, which has provided vital information, the panels were already in the palace in 1678».

(30) Ramalho Ortigão, *A Arte e a Natureza em Portugal*.
(31) Ernesto de Campos de Andrada, *O Palácio dos Marqueses de Fonteira e os seus manuscritos*, «Revista de História», Year XII, N.s 47 and 48, p. 245.
(32) Ernesto de Campos de Andrada, *Op. cit.*, p. 246.
(33) «Guia de Portugal», *Op. cit.*, p. 297.
(34) Júlio de Castilho, *A Ribeira de Lisboa*, p. 178.
(35) I found several leases in the Palácio Fronteira archives for the «land in Chagas» where the primitive palace had once stood, one of which said the following: «Let it be known that this lease with guaranty and bond in the year of Our Lord eighteen hundred and twenty four on the nineteenth day of the month of February in the city of Lisbon and in S. Domingos Square where I, the Notary, came to the house in which resides the most illustrious Dr. Rafael Ignacio Pimenta, lawyer of the Casa da Suplicação who is present as Procurator for His Excellency the Marquis of Fronteira. A copy of the procuration was presented, and will be kept in this registry's archives; for the other side is Francisco de Salles e Oliveira residing in Chagas number six, Parish of Santa Catherina represents his mother, Maria Tereza de Oliveira, widow of António Pedro de Oliveira which was proven in the procuration shown, which will also be kept in this registry's archives. Dr. Rafael Ignacio Pimenta said that His Excellency the Marquis of Fronteira, his client and Lord and owner of the land mentioned in the Chagas where the residential palace of his forefathers had once stood, and which had burnt down in the earthquake of first November of seventeen hundred and fifty five; this land was rented to the above Maria Tereza de Oliveira for the annual fee of two hundred and twenty thousand Reis free of tax to His Excellency and paid in advance, until December eighteen hundred and twenty three: And as His Excellency was asked to continue the same lease for another six years, beginning on January first of the present year of eighteen hundred and twenty four and ending on thirty first of December of eighteen hundred and twenty

nino for the same price and conditions His Excellency having no doubt that he would continue with the same lease due to the punctuality with which the payments had always been and hoped would continue being paid...etc.» and so this contract continues having incorporated the respective procurations and a few articles at the end, one of which I would like to show: the contract is revoked «if they should want to rebuild the Palace on the above mentioned land they have the right to do so and Maria Tereza de Oliveira is compelled to give back the land, being thus warned by His Excellence that in this case he would be obliged to pay eighty thousand reis for each year until the end of this six year contract, according to the Law...»

Not all the lands on the Chagas belonged to the Marquis of Fronteira, as there was a part that was free and another that had a long lease, there is a deed dated 11th June, 1802 in the Fronteira Archives in which the Marquis acknowledges the long lease to the Patriarchal Basilica of Santa Maria in the same terms as for the Palácio das Chagas.

(36) Ramalho Ortigão, *Op. cit.*

(37) Gabriel Pereira, *Op. cit.*, p. 34.

(38) Alfredo Mesquita, *Portugal Pitoresco e Ilustrado*, p. 43.

(39) Jorge de Moser, *Op. cit.*, p. 183.

(40) The tenth Count of Torre inherited this palace from his aunt, D. Leonor Mascarenhas, on the occasion of his marriage to the Marchioness of Ávila and Bolama in 1924.

(41) Gabriel Pereira, *Op. cit.*, p. 48.

(42) Inácio de Vilhena Barbosa, *Monumentos de Portugal*, p. 496.

(43) Ramalho Ortigão, *Op. cit.*

(44) Ramalho Ortigão, *Op. cit.*

[45] George Kubler, *A Arquitectura Portuguesa Chã entre as Especiarias e os Diamantes*, Lisboa, 1989.

[46] Marquês de Ávila e de Bolama, *Nova Carta Corográfica de Portugal*, vol. III, p. 359.

(47) This stone adorned with the coats of arms, placed here by the eleventh Count of Torre, was removed from a building, at the time owned by the House of Fronteira, in the Praça D. Pedro IV (Rossio — Lisbon) where the Café Chave d'Ouro now stands.

(48) Marquês de Ávila e de Bolama, *Op. cit.*, p. 359.

(49) Marquês de Ávila e de Bolama, *Op. cit.*, p. 359.

(50) Ernesto de Campos de Andrada, *Op. cit*, p. 244.

(51) Luis Teixeira de Sampaio, *Os Chavões*, «Revista de História», N.º 36, p. 307.

(52) José Queirós, *Op. cit.*, p. 237.

[53] J. M. dos Santos Simões, *Azulejaria em Portugal no Século xvii*, 2nd edition, 1990, t. II, p. 107.

(54) This room had very unfortunate works of restoration done in 1915 by the second Marquises of Ávila and Bolama who left the following inscription:«Restored in 1915 by Dona Leonor Maria Mascarenhas and António José de Ávila, second Marquises of Ávila and Bolama who inherited this house from their first cousin Dona Maria Mascarenhas Barreto, eighth Marchioness of Fronteira and sixth Marchioness of Alorna ».

(55/56) Esteves Pereira and Guilherme Rodrigues, *Portugal* (historical dictionary), vol. II, p. 286. On this matter the authors of this dictionary added the following: «They say that the helmet worn by Dom João of Austria in that battle, showing the mark of the second Count of Torre's sword, is in the Royal Armoury of Madrid».

(57) The eleventh Count of Torre had these tiles, signed by Gabriel Constante and made in 1925, put here.

(58) Gabriel Pereira, *Op. cit.*, p. 33.

(59) Ernesto de Campos de Andrada, *Op. cit.*, p. 247.

(60) Ernesto de Campos de Andrada, *Op. cit.*, p. 246.

(61) Ernesto de Campos de Andrada, *Op. cit.*, p. 249.

[62] J. M. dos Santos Simões, *Op. cit.*, p. 106.

[63] This distinguished lady painted, [besides a drawing in pastel done in Viena, Austria, representing Solitude, a self-portrait which she gave to her father to show how much she missed him] another picture representing Married Love and offered it to the Princess of Brazil, Dona Maria Benedita. This painting and others and also several drawings were burnt in the fire at the Palácio da Ajuda. In this same room there is a drawing in pencil of the head of the executed Marchioness of Távora, also made by Alcipe.

(64) Domingos Pellegrini, the Italian painter stayed in Portugal from 1803 to 1810 when he was forced to leave the country by the Government (Sousa Viterbo, «News of some Portuguese painters and other foreign ones who practiced their art in Portugal»). For further knowledge, I would like to add the following about this painter :

«Senza dubbio Domenico Pellegrini, nato a Galliera di Bassano nel 1759 e morto a Roma nel 1840, é il pittore straniero piú interessante e notevole che sia arrivato in Portogallo nei primi anni del secolo XIX... Quando, ancora giovane, Domenico Pellegrini andò a Roma, sembra vi frequentasse lo studio di Domenico Corvi, accademizzante correttissimo pittore. Nello studio del Corvi faceva allora le sue esperienze Domenico Antonio de Sequeira, che poi rimase legato d'amicizia col Pellegrini. Questi tuttavia, se poteva interessarsi al modo di comporre e disegnare del Corvi, non doveva, certo, amare quei suoi colorini dolciastri che avevano pretese quasi veneziane, lui che di colore veneto se ne intendeva.

Dopo Roma, il Pellegrini andò a Parigi e a Londra, dove ebbe occasione di conoscere il marchese di Belas, al quale dipinse il ritratto assieme alla famiglia.

Fu forse in quella occasione che il Pellegrini ricevette l'invito di recarsi in Portogallo, e nel 1803 giunse a Lisbona, dove ebbe subito un grande sucesso...

Furono allora numerosissimi i ritratti da lui dipinti per i personaggi delle famiglie in composizioni complesse ma piene di decoro, come quel grande quadro, in casa del marchese di Fronteira a Benfica, nel quale ritrasse il marchese Alorna circondato dai suoi famigliari...» (Emilio Lavagnino, *L'Opera Del Genio Italiano All'Estero*, «Gli Artisti in Portogallo», pp. 140 and 141).

(65) One of the most famous generals of his time. He participated in the campaigns of 1793, 1794 and 1795 in Roussillon and in Catalunha and in 1801 against the Spaniards. As commander in chief of the Portuguese Legion (nominated on 1st August, 1808), he accompanied Napoleon in the Russian campaigns, «he died of homesickness, cold and hunger» in Koenigsberg on 2nd January, 1813. The Marchioness was the daughter of the sixth Counts of S. Vicente.

(66) Ramalho Ortigão, *Op. cit.*

(67) It has been said that due to some misfortune the frescos on the ceiling had to be painted again.

(68) Ernesto de Campos de Andrada, *Op. cit.*, p. 246.

(69) Inácio de Vilhena Barbosa, *Monumentos de Portugal*, p. 496.

(70) Ramalho Ortigão, *Op. cit.*

(71) Marquês de Ávila e de Bolama, *Op. cit.*, vol. III, p. 366.

(72) Luís Teixeira de Sampaio, *Op. cit.*, p. 307.

(73) Gabriel Pereira, *Op. cit.*, p. 48.

[74] Gabriel Pereira, *Op. cit.*, p. 48.

[75] Lúcio de Azevedo, *Os Jesuitas no Grão Pará*, p. 38.

[76] Schaeffer, *História de Portugal*, vol. III, p. 366.

[77] Schaeffer, *Op. cit.*, vol. III, p. 366.

(78) Besides the gardens, one must recall the quinta which in time had been a remarkable orange grove. I found several notes in the Palácio archives with different dates and illegible signatures. One, dated 1383, speaks of the «Income of the buildings in the parish of Benfica owned by His Excellency the Marquis of Fronteira and which I administer» concerning the second half of that year. As to the Palácio he says: «Palácio with all the workhouses, lofts, stables and coach houses, garden, orchard, vineyard, fruit trees and some vegetables, the produce of this month is the oranges which were sold for two hundred and twenty thousand reis, the vegetables were for home consumption could have been worth nine thousand six hundred reis, we can calculate the average 200.000 for the oranges comparing to previous years considering the decrease of this product».

(79) José Queirós, *Op. cit.*, p. 237.

(80) Ernesto de Campos de Andrada, *Op. cit.*, p. 243.

(81) Gabriel Pereira, *Op. cit.*, p. 35.

(82) Ramalho Ortigão, *Op. cit.*

(83) All, or a great many writers who have referred to these tiles state that the twelve men at the front represent the Doze de Inglaterra and the ones at each side are two Mascarenhas. This tradition of the Doze de Inglaterra is interesting and originated one of the most beautiful parts of the Lusiadas but, in my opinion, it has nothing to do with the figures represented here. Everything I have written and will do so in the future confirms my opinion. Why would the Doze de Inglaterra appear here?

(84) Jorge de Moser, *Op. cit.*, p. 186.

(85) Ramalho Ortigão, *Op. cit.*

(86) José Queirós, *Op. cit.*, p. 236.

(87) Gabriel Pereira, *Op. cit.*, p. 37.

(88) Nicolau Tolentino, *Obras Completas*, by J. Torres, 1861, p. 246.

[89] Gabriel Pereira, *Op. cit.*, p. 31.

(90) José Queirós, *Op. cit.*, p. 237.

(91) It is difficult to mention every member of this family who fought there, so I will only mention the Viceroys: Dom Pedro Mascarenhas (6th Viceroy, 1554-1555); Dom Francisco Mascarenhas (13th Viceroy, 1581-1584); Dom Filipe Mascarenhas (26th Viceroy, 1645-1651); Dom Vasco Mascarenhas (27th Viceroy, 1652-1655); Dom Manuel Mascarenhas (4th council); Dom Pedro Mascarenhas (42nd Viceroy, 1732-1741); and Dom Luís Mascarenhas (46th Viceroy, 1754-1756). What it was to be Viceroy of India is well explained below:

«The Viceroy residing in his palace, the House of Sabayo, or later known as Palácio da Fortaleza, surrounded by a court, receiving the Ambassadors of Shah of Persia, of the King of Cambaya, of the Adil Shah or from the Rajah of Bijayanagra, equal to the most powerful in the East, he used well this extraordinary power which the Portuguese had quickly conquered by the bravery and audacity and at the cost of a great loss of blood, theirs and of their enemies». Count of Ficalho, *Garcia da Horta e o seu Tempo*, p. 148.

(92) Five governors were proposed by Dom Henrique: Jorge de Almeida, archbishop of Lisbon; Francisco de Sáda, Lord Chamberlain of the Kindom; João Tellez, João Mascarenhas and Diogo Lopes de Sousa, president of the capital's Court of Justice. Schaeffer, *Op. cit.*, vol. III, p. 423.

(93) Diogo de Couto, Decade VI, book VI, chap. VII, p. 50.

(94) Afonso de Dornelas, *Elucidario Nobiliarchico*, vol. I, p. 276.

(95) Bettencourt, *Descobrimentos, guerras e conquistas dos portugueses em terras do ultramar nos séculos xv e xvi*, p. 189 (Biblioteca Nacional de Lisboa. Reservados 9220).

(96) Gaspar Correia, *Lendas da Índia*, 1st serie, t. II, p. 305.

(97) Bettencourt, *Op. cit.*, pp. 199 and 200. (Biblioteca Nacional de Lisboa, Reservados 9220).

António Galvão, *Tratado dos descobrimentos antigos e modernos feitos até à Era de 1550*, p. 51, Biblioteca Nacional de Lisboa, vol. 2734).

(98) Padre José de Castro, *Portugal no Concílio de Trento*, vol. I, pp. 279 and 280.

(99) Augusto Cardoso Pinto, *A Guarda del Rei D. João II*, p. 71.

(100) José Ferreira Martins, *Os Vice-Reis da Índia*, pp. 71 and 72.

(101) Biblioteca Nacional de Lisboa. Reservados 979, *Nobiliário de D. António de Lima*, Título dos Mascarenhas, p. 251.

(102) Teófilo Braga, *História da Universidade de Coimbra*, t. I, p. 287; António Sardinha, *A Lareira de Castela*, 2nd edition, p. 161; William Thomas Walsh, *Filipe II*, 3rd Spanish edition, p. 32.

(103) M. Gachard, *Don Carlos et Philipe II*, Paris, 1867, p. 5.

(104) Diogo Barbosa Machado, *Biblioteca Lusitana*, 2nd edition, t. II, p. 31. Fortunato de Almeida, *História da Igreja em Portugal*, t. III, part II, p. 894.

(105) *Account of what happened at the proclamation of the Almighty King João IV*, printed in 1641.

(106) José Silvestre Ribeiro, *História dos Estabelecimentos Scientificos, Litterarios e Artisticos de Portugal*, t. IV, p. 197.

(107) *Account of what happened at the proclamation of the Almighty King João IV*, printed in 1641.

(108) D. Francisco Manuel de Melo, *Tacito Português, Vida e Morte, Ditos e Feitos de El-Rei D. João IV*, Rio de Janeiro, 1940, p. 54.

(109) These nobles would meet in Jorge de Melo's house in Xabregas and all the decisions made there were transmitted to Dr. João Pinto Ribeiro. *História de Portugal, de Barcelos*, fasc. 58, p. 274.

(110) *História de Portugal, de Barcelos*, fasc. 58, p. 274.

(111) *Account of what happened at the proclamation of the Almighty King João IV*, printed in 1641.

(112) *História de Portugal, de Barcelos*, fasc. 58, p. 275.

(113/114) *Account of what happened at the proclamation of the Almighty King João IV*, printed in 1641.

(115) *História de la Ciudade de Ceuta*, written by D. Jerónimo Mascarenhas, edited by Academia das Ciências de Lisboa under the direction of Afonso de Dornelas, pp. IX and following.

(116) Rocha Martins, *Os Grandes Vultos da Restauração de Portugal*, pp. 251 and 252.

(117) To specify the privileges of the Priors of Crato would take up too much space, however as an example, they owned thirteen villages: Crato, S. João de Gafete, Tolosa, Amieira, Gavião, Belver, Envendos, Carvoeiro, Proença-a-Nova, Sertã, Pedrógão Pequeno or of Crato, Oleiros and Álvaro. The Crato Priory was permanently joined to the Casa do Infantado by charter on 31st January, 1790. The first prior was Friar Álvaro Gonçalves Pereira, father of the Condestável Nuno Álvares Pereira and amongst others, also of Prince Luís, King Pedro III and Prince João. *História dos Estabelecimentos Sci-*

entíficos, Literários e Artísticos de Portugal, vol. III, p. 88.

(118) Diogo de Barbosa Machado, *Biblioteca Lusitana, história, crítica e cronológica*, t. IV. In the Patriarchal workshop of Francisco Luís Ameno, p. 184. On the same subject it also states: «These works were kept in the library belonging to João Caetano de Mello dos Povos».

(119) Augusto Cardoso Pinto, *Catálogo dos Capitães-mores dos Ginetes e dos Capitães da Guarda Del Rei*, p. 42.

(120) Augusto Cardoso Pinto, *Op. cit.*, pp. 44 and 46.

(121) Augusto Cardoso Pinto, *Op. cit.*, pp. 44 and 46.

(122) Augusto Cardoso Pinto, *Op. cit.*, pp. 44 and 46.

(123) This rank produced the name of a street in Lisbon, «rua do Capitão dos Ginetes which passed under the arch joining the noble Mascarenhas and Mellos houses which became known as the Arch of the Capitão dos Ginetes...», it was joined by a row of buildings to the fourth quarter of Trindade or André Soares. «Three buildings faced the rua do Capitão dos Ginetes», belonging, in 1554, to Dom Pedro Mascarenhas, sixth Viceroy of India, son of Fernam Martins Mascarenhas. Matos Sequeira, *O Carmo e a Trindade*, vol.I, pp. 220 and 241.

(124) Augusto Cardoso Pinto, *Catálogo dos Capitães-mores dos Ginetes e dos Capitães da Guarda del Rei*, p. 20.

(125) Garcia de Resende, *Crónica de D. João II*, quoted by Augusto Cardoso Pinto in *A Guarda del Rei D. João II*, p. 60.

(126) Anselmo Braamcamp Freire, *As Sepulturas do Espinheiro*, p. 4. They are thirty two quatrains, «slanderous ballads», dedicated to people who frequented the Court, at the time, the anonymous author finished off with the following interesting quatrain:

C'os porquês deveys folguar,
poys que a ninguem impece:
e rria quem se alegrar,

e quem nam va-sse beyjar
onde lha'a pelle fallece.

(127) Rui de Pina, *Crónica de D. João II*, quoted by Anselmo Braamcamp Freire in *As Sepulturas do Espinheiro*, p. 3.

(128) Anselmo Braamcamp Freire, *Op. cit.*, p. 2.

(129) Fortunato de Almeida, *Op. cit.*, t. III, part II, p. 565.

(130) Conde de Campo Bello, *Governadores Gerais e Vice-Reis do Brasil*, p. 63.

(131) Consiglieri Sá Pereira, *A Restauração Vista de Espanha*, p. 90.

(132) Dom Diogo de Eça who owned his parents house — Quinta dos Torres — in Azeitão was shot dead in the Calçada do Combro (Lisbon) for having killed Dom Manuel Mascarenhas, as can be seen on page XX, on 7th February, 1649, when he refused to marry his sister Dona Luísa, who inherited the Quinta dos Torres. *Nobres Casas de Portugal*, vol. I, p. 129.

(133) Padre Manuel Bernardes, *Nova Floresta*, edited by Library Chardron, vol. I, p. 432.

(134) Rocha Martins, *Op. cit*, p. 326.

(135) *Monstruosidades do Tempo e da Fortuna*. New edition under the direction of Damião Peres, vol. i, p. 76 and vol. IV, p. 50.

(136) Diogo Barbosa Machado, *Biblioteca Lusitana*, 2nd edition, t. II, p. 34.

(137) Diogo Barbosa Machado, *Biblioteca Lusitana*, 2nd edition, t. II, p. 34.

(138) D. António Caetano de Sousa, *História Genealógica*, t. IX, p. 468.

(139) *Memórias do Marquês de Fronteira e d'Alorna*, vol. I, p. 12. *A Descendência Portuguesa de El-rei D. João II*, by Fernando Carredo, vol. II, *Condes de Conculim*, p. 162.

(140) Dona Leonor de Almeida Portugal de Lorena e Lencastre, on the death of her brother, the general, third Marquis of Alorna, inherited the assets and titles from the House of Alorna, by marriage, Countess of Oyenhausen-Gravenbourg in Austria, one of the most remarkable Portuguese women who, aged eight, entered the Convent of Chelas with her mother and sister when her father was put in the Junqueira prison, they were only allowed to leave on the death of King José, eighteen years later. There she spent most of her youth, always studying and at the age of sixteen some of her compositions became known and word of her talen began to spread. At this time Francisco Manuel do Nascimento, known as Filinto Elísio, went to the Convent of Chelas with some friends and immortalized the fourth Marchioness of Alorna naming her Alcipe, which was how she was known from then on to all Portuguese poets. After her marriage she frequented the courts of King Carlos III of Spain; King Louis XVI of France, Emperess Maria Teresa of Vienna, in Paris she was an habitué of Mr. Necker's house, father of Mme. de Stael, meeting place for the intellectuals and politicians of the time. She left a remarkable work of poetry, part of it published in six volumes in 1844, and a lot of correspondence of great historical interest unpublished.
Professor Hernani Cidade in «Colecção de Clássicos Sá da Costa», dedicated two volumes to her work. The first has a selection of poetry and the second the correspondence in which all her political activity is dealt with and is composed exclusively of unpublished manuscripts from the Fronteira archives.
There are innumerable works from abroad which refer to her and Alexandre Herculano in *Panorama* writes of her in the following way: «...that extraordinary woman had she belonged to another country other than this poor little forgotten Portugal, would have become one the most brilliant proof against vain pretentions of the excessive superiority of our sex. She gave me incentive and literary protection when I was still in my youth and taking my first steps on the road of words...».

(141) With the joining of the Houses of Alorna and Fronteira the titles of Marquises of Távora and Counts of S. João da Pesqueira as well as the other titles of the illustrious house were incorporated in the latter.

(142) *Memórias do Marquês de Fronteira e d'Alorna*, vol. II, p. 144.